Brave Faces
with
Broken Hearts

An Autobiography by
Kelly Farrelly

To Wendy Love From Kelly farrelly x.

ISBN No. 978-1-907636-15-8

Published by Verité

Cover design, typesetting and production management by
Verité CM Ltd, Worthing, West Sussex UK
www.veritecm.com

Dedication

This book is dedicated to my dearly loved mother, Maureen McRae,
a woman who showed me what being a Christian really means;
a woman now at peace with our Lord Jesus Christ.

Acknowledgements

I would like to thank the following people,
for their faithfulness, love and support.
They have held my hand every step of the way:

My precious husband who gave his life to Jesus Christ.
My wonderful children, Luke, Matthew, Grace, and Hope,
who behaved well so that I could spend time to write this book.
My dad, my best friend
My auntie and sister in Christ, Eileen Brown
My sister in Christ and friend, Carole Martins, Aguiar
My beloved friends Lou Ilmisen and Ayse Dalyanoglu,
Chi Chi Ohuonu who typed the manuscript, Udoka Ohuonu who
edited it and Rachael Hobbs who edited and laid out the pages.
Without them this book would not have happened.
My thanks to my publisher Chris Powell who believed in my vision

Thank you so much. I love you all.

There is a love to be found that can heal the most broken heart;
a love and sincere love that will never fail you or leave you.

I write this book for everyone who has had a broken heart.
To tell them there is hope and there is love to be found, a real love
that's true and sincere; a love that will never leave you or fail you.

For the protection of others, the names and identities of people in
this book have been changed.

Part One

I was born, the youngest of three children in 1975 in Park Head, Glasgow. My dad was Scottish and my mum was a Glaswegian of Irish descent.

I was only a few weeks old when word spread in the city that an aluminium factory was due to be built in the Highlands of Scotland. My dad had worked the Barras Lands markets in the east end of Glasgow for many years and decided he didn't want to bring us up in the city. He applied for a job at the new factory, which was in a small village called Invergordon. It was a quick process and I was only four weeks old when we left Glasgow to start our new life there.

Invergordon is a small village by the sea. The population eventually grew to about three and a half thousand people, but at the time we moved there were no houses and we lived in a caravan on the land where the aluminium factory was being built. It was known as the Invergordon Smelter.

Work was plentiful and council estates were built as more people were drawn to the area for work. Everyone living on the caravan site was allocated a house by the council and we eventually moved into a small three bedroom one.

We lived in a small community and knew everybody. People were polite, friendly and always cheerful willing to make time for a chat. Most parents were strict and we always had to be polite and well behaved. We were taught right from wrong and would get a good smack on the backside if we were cheeky. As a family, we didn't have much but there was always enough to eat. Most importantly of all, there was love.

Although my parents were together I never really knew my dad. Mum stayed at home and looked after us. She was the one who made the house homely and warm. She fed us, cleaned us and was always there to talk to. Mum took us to school and picked us up and I always loved to see her at the end of the school day. She would often take us to the sweet shop and walk us home along the sea front.

I had so much love for her, probably because we spent so much time together. She would always tell me that she loved me and that I was special.

Dad was a real grafter, working every hour he could to put food on the table. Although we didn't know him well, we had great respect for him. He expected us to respect his wishes but this wasn't demonstrated in an unkind or abusive way and we understood that 'No' meant no and there was no way to change his mind. Dad would come home in the evening after a hard day's work and want his dinner, a bath and a bit of peace and quiet, as such we would be sent upstairs to bed shortly after dad came home.

My brother, sister and I would always strive to be good when he was home as he would ask mum if we had been good and would be cross if we hadn't.

One day when I was six years old, something happened that had never happened before; dad came to pick us up from school. I was confused and terrified that something had happened to Mum as Dad didn't say anything to begin with and he had a worried look on his face. He told us that mum had been in hospital to have an operation to remove her womb and that he had come to collect us and take us to see her.

Dad always tried not to worry us and my brother, sister and I were often sent outside to play so that he and mum could talk. They had been doing this a lot recently and it was then that we found out that mum had cancer of the womb. I didn't understand what that meant, or even what cancer was but dad assured us that she was fine and would be home in a few days.

"Dad always tried not to worry us"

Dad took us to the hospital in Inverness and my first impression wasn't a good one. I didn't like it at all and just wanted to go, taking mum with me. Mum had never left us before and I remember crying as she wasn't able to come home with us. When she was eventually able to come home I clung to her side, I just wanted to be with her all the time. I was terrified that she would have to go back to the hospital and leave me again.

We didn't have much money so I didn't have swimming or dancing lessons. As such, most of my childhood years were spent playing on the streets of the council estate, climbing trees, playing in the park, or playing in the forest behind our house. As we grew older we were allowed to cross the roads by ourselves and play further from home. I loved wandering around seeing what other people were doing.

Despite those happy times playing with friends, the fear of Mum's cancer was always with me. I didn't understand what cancer was, neither did I understand why Mum would walk along the sea front and pop into the church to say a prayer.

Our school holidays would be spent in Glasgow visiting our aunts, uncles and cousins. We found them funny because they spoke with a different accent to us and they would laugh at the way we spoke and call us 'highlanders chuchtors'. When I was older, Mum would often send me to stay with relatives on my own in the summer holidays. I found out that these were the times when she had to go into hospital.

The constant fear that my mum would have to go back into hospital made me feel sick with worry. The thought of her dying scared me intensely and I lived with that fear throughout my childhood. I had no interest in studying and didn't try to get good grades; Mum needed my help at home and I felt I was wasting my time at school.

Life was much the same when I started secondary school. We still lived on the council estate in Invergordon, Mum's cancer was in remission and Dad's working pattern was the same as before. He worked hard and spent any spare time with my brother at football training as he was becoming known in the Highlands for being a really good footballer. My relationship with Dad hadn't changed at all; Mum was still my main carer and the one I turned to for everything.

"I loved my mum so much"

I loved my mum so much that I always wanted to go wherever she went. She loved going to church so I loved to go with her. Sometimes she would walk along the sea front and pop in to the church to say a prayer. I used to sit and watch as she would get on her knees and pray. To me it was strange that she was talking to someone she couldn't see.

'It helps me stay strong and get through the cancer,' she would say. 'I said a prayer for you Kelly.'

'You don't need to pray for me,' I would say, 'I'm okay.

As time passed Mum became ill again. It was never really spoken about, but we learned that the cancer had spread to her breast and she had to go to hospital to have the breast removed. I could see the fear in her face and asked if I could go with her.

I watched the tears run down her face. Deep down she was petrified but she tried to stay strong. She had lost her mum to cancer and was afraid to leave us without a mother. That broke her heart more than the cancer and I couldn't bear to see her sadness.

After Mum's operation Dad took us to see her. As we pulled up at the hospital I could feel hatred welling up inside me. I hated hospitals! I only ever had bad memories of them. As we went in I could smell the hospital smell which made me feel sick. Trolleys clanging down the corridors, sickly looking old people. I wanted to leave as soon as possible.

As we entered the ward I could see that Mum didn't look good; tears filled my eyes. I tried to hold them back but I just couldn't. Mum was still under the effects of the anaesthetic. As I looked around the ward all I could see were old people who looked like they were dying. 'Is this what is going to happen to my mum? Is this what cancer does?' I thought. I left the hospital petrified at the thought that my mum might die.

That night I lay in the bed and sobbed my heart out. I cried out to God, 'Please God let my mum live, I'm begging you!' Many nights after that I cried myself to sleep each night begging God not to take my mum away.

The weeks passed and Mum gradually recovered. Dad took on a job working night shifts so that he could look after Mum during the day. He was amazing in the way he looked after her. I still stayed close to Mum and would listen to her as she said her prayers every night. She would always pray for me and I couldn't understand why she felt that she needed to because I thought I was okay.

Mum and Dad spent every penny they had on transport to and from the hospital for Mum's checkups. I didn't realise how tight money had become and one day I asked for a new pair of trainers. It was the 'in thing' at that time to have Nike trainers. 'I can't buy you shoes; I can't afford them right now,' Mum said crying. I walked out of the room, crying myself for having upset mum over a pair of shoes. I hated myself for it.

I decided to get a job. I was thirteen and felt old enough to work. I asked people I knew on the estate and started babysitting. I also started working in the local farm shop after school. I liked having money and I began buying little gifts for Mum. I wanted to work in order to buy her nice things but Mum wouldn't take the money.

'Save your money you might need it,' she said, 'I may not be here one day and you will have to look after yourself.'

I was frightened by her words. 'What do you mean?' I asked.

'The cancer could come back and I could die,' she replied.

'Don't say that,' I'd say.

I finally saved enough money to buy my first pair of Nike trainers. I felt very grown up and responsible, being able to buy clothes and shoes for myself. I disliked school and felt that I was wasting my time there when I could be working and earning money.

Although I still carried the worry of Mum's cancer, she was looking well that I believed she was going to be okay. Dad was now running the local football club and my brother was doing well at football. Everyone was happy.

My first encounter with God

Mum had a friend who had been told her about an evangelist who had started a church in the next village. She invited Mum to go and I said that I wanted to go too. Her friend picked us up and we went to the next village to see what the church was all about. As a child I had always been curious about different churches and Mum and I attended many of them so that I could see what they were like.

As we went inside, we realised that this church was very different to any of the other churches we'd ever been to. One man was dancing and clapping; Mum and I had never seen anything like that in church before and couldn't stop laughing! We laughed so hard that tears came out of our eyes. We thought that the man was a bit of a lunatic, but most of the people had happy faces and really seemed to be enjoying themselves.

Mum and I enjoyed ourselves too, even though we were not quite sure about the happy-clappy man. Everyone chatted to us afterwards and they seemed nice and friendly. As the weeks passed, Mum and I continued to attend.

The evangelist started a Bible study group during the week and asked if I'd like to go. I really wanted to, as it was a chance to meet other young people. I enjoyed going and it was great fun to meet kids from another village. The evangelist told us about a youth rally that was being held in Dunfermline and wanted to take the group. I was so excited; I had only ever been to Glasgow and I really wanted to go. Mum agreed immediately, Dad wasn't so sure but Mum persuaded him that I'd be fine.

I don't remember much about the preacher at the rally. All I recall was him saying 'Would anyone like to give their life to Jesus Christ?' I put my hand up straight away. I didn't really understand what it all meant but I knew that I wanted to give my life to Jesus. I remember his words: 'Come forward for prayer if you want to give your life to Jesus and do God's will.' I did; I felt so excited. I rushed to the front and someone was standing there praying for all the young people. One moment I was standing and the next I fell back and lay flat on the floor for a few minutes. I remember standing up again, strange words coming out of my mouth. As I was standing the same thing happened and I fell back again.

"I knew that I wanted to give my life to Jesus"

I spoke to the evangelist, who explained that I had spoken in 'tongues', a heavenly language. Wow, it felt great! I couldn't wait to tell Mum what had happened. God was real and had really touched my life. I felt so happy.

We had to stay the night in Clydebank, Glasgow, so I didn't return home until late the next day. Mum saw the excitement on my face and listened to my story. 'Are you sure?' she said.

'Yes,' I replied. 'It was amazing!' Mum telephoned my aunt in Glasgow to tell her what had happened. She had not heard of this happening to anyone before.

We went back to the church on Sunday evening and the same thing happened to me again. Mum couldn't believe what she saw. Something amazing had happened but we didn't really understand what it was or what the experience meant.

Mum had always been a smoker. Straight after the service, she and some of the other members of the congregation went outside for a cigarette. As the evangelist came out he made a comment about them smoking. Some of those who had been smoking with mum denied it. Mum couldn't believe it and was very angry. 'Hypocrites', she called them and that was the last time she attended that church. She forbade me from going too.

A lot of people had been unsure about the evangelist and when members of the church tried to contact us my dad told them to leave us alone. Dad told us to keep away from the church. He used the tone of voice that told you he meant what he said. We didn't hear anymore from the evangelist or the other members of the church.

Now I had nothing to look forward to. I had always enjoyed going to church on Sunday evening, as it was the one place where I could forget about Mum's cancer. There was absolutely nothing to do in our village. I was now very bored and very fed up.

A new escape

Mum was deteriorating fast. Day by day I watched her life drain away. She kept a brave face and tried her best not to upset us, but I would see the heartache on her face and the tears of frustration rolling down her cheeks.

Day after day I would sit by Mum's bedside or cuddle up with her in bed. I didn't want to leave her; school was unbearable as I was petrified she would die whilst I was away.

To cheer her up I would tell her that I would make her proud one day: 'I'll go to South Africa. I'll work hard, get rich and make something of my life.' This would bring a smile to her face. 'Save your money,' she would say, 'I'll be gone one day you will be on your own. You will need it to look after yourself.' Her words terrified me.

Mum asked me to stay a virgin until I got married and I promised I would. I had no interest in boyfriends. Spending time with my friends and earning money was what I loved to do.

One day I called for my friend Katie and we wandered down to the High Street. We were only there for a short while when Dad drove past. Seeing me, he stopped the car and shouted at me to get in. 'I told you I didn't want you hanging out on the High Street,' he shouted. I wanted to curl up in a ball and hide. I felt so humiliated as I got into the car, tears of anger and frustration burning my eyes. When we got home I was warned to stay away from the High Street. He said the street was full of boys driving up and down looking for young girls, people selling drugs and people getting drunk.

I was determined to sneak down there again without Dad knowing. This wasn't like me, but I wasn't going to let him humiliate me. I'd never lied to my parents before but I told Dad that I was just going out to spend time with friends on the estate. After leaving the house I headed straight to the High Street to find Katie. I knew I was betraying my dad but I was angry and didn't care. I finally found Katie. 'You're crazy,' she said. 'If your dad catches you, you're done for.'

'He won't,' I said, and we both burst out laughing. It was the first time that I had laughed in a long time. I realised that I got a buzz of excitement from being rebellious and getting the better of Dad.

I watched people coming out of the pub. They were laughing and singing, full of excitement. I realised that I wanted to be happy like that. I didn't want to be burdened with worry anymore. I wanted to be a teenager, to laugh and have fun. I wanted an escape from all the sadness I was hiding deep down inside.

I decided that alcohol would become my escape. As Katie and I walked home, we decided that the following Friday we would put our money together and buy some alcohol. 'Let's get drunk,' I said. At last I had something to look forward to; I was excited at the thought of getting drunk.

I arrived home and Dad didn't say a word to me. As I sat on the floor beside Mum's bed, I thought of our plan for Friday but knew I could only go if she didn't need me. 'I might go out with Katie Friday if you feel okay,' I said to Mum.

'I can't bear to see you so sad,' she replied, 'Go and enjoy yourself. I can have time on my own with your dad.'

Friday finally arrived and I had butterflies in my stomach all day.

I had looked forward to this all week. Although I was afraid of what would happen if my dad found out, the excitement took the fear away. If getting drunk made everyone else happy, I was sure it would make me happy too.

Katie and I knew we were too young to go into the off-licence. We had gotten to know an older guy called Mark who always stood on the corner and we plucked up the courage to ask him to buy us some alcohol. 'What do you want?' he asked us.

We didn't have a clue. 'You better not tell anyone I got this for you or I'll be done for,' he warned. 'Promise if you get caught by the police, you won't say it was me or I'll never help you again.'

'We won't,' we promised.

Mark went into the off licence and came out with a bottle of Bucks Fast. Katie and I were both afraid that we would get caught so we decided to hide in the school. She took the first swig and grimaced. Then it was my turn; I took a swig from the bottle and spat it straight out. It tasted disgusting. After a few more mouthfuls we started to get used to the taste. Although it didn't taste as nice as we had thought it would, it gave us a strange sensation as it trickled down our throats. We started laughing and I began to feel dizzy. I wasn't thinking of mum and for the first time since I'd stopped attending the church service in the next village, I felt happy. We finished the bottle and headed back towards the High Street. I felt great; it gave me the confidence to talk to the other people who were hanging around. It was starting to get late so we decided to go home. We joined arms and sang silly songs all the way back. We had had fun and it felt great to laugh again.

The following week I continued with my babysitting jobs and went to work in the farm shop. Mum was doing okay and didn't need me to help her. She wanted some quiet time with dad so once again it was no problem for me to go out with Katie.

On Friday night, we couldn't wait to get to the High Street. Mark was standing on the street corner as usual. He went into the off-licence and bought some cider for us. This was much better than the Bucks Fast. It tasted nicer and made us gigglier; I felt great.

I sat on the wall watching people singing and shouting, going from pub to pub. I found it funny watching people stumbling about drunk.

Suddenly everyone came rushing out the pubs, shouting with excitement, 'The boogie bus is coming!' They all rushed up the street as fast they could and got on the bus. We asked Mark what it was all about. He told us that a new night club had opened in a place called Dingwall which was a half hour drive from the village. 'Oh well', I thought to myself, 'I'll have to wait until I'm eighteen.'

As I lay in bed that night all I could think about was the night club in Dingwall. I was now regularly telling lies to my parents in order to hang out on the High Street so I didn't feel bad about lying in order to go to the nightclub. I just wanted to be able to laugh and scream, to sing and shout and to have fun like everyone else was. I knew that Katie's mum would not

"I was now regularly telling lies to my parents."

allow her to go as we were only fifteen so I need a different plan. I had another friend, Laura who was more daring and her parents weren't as strict as Katie's. I decided to ask her to go with me.

I spoke to Laura at school on Monday morning. 'You're mad,' she said, 'we have our exams.'

At that point in time I couldn't care less about my exams. I didn't like going to school and had very little time for my teachers. They were part of the reason that I had no interest in school as they showed very little interest in students who weren't obviously clever. I spoke to Laura again at lunchtime and managed to convince her to come to Dingwall with me. We spent the week planning so that we would be able to go out without being caught.

On Friday evening I told Mum and Dad that I was staying at Laura's house. We bought some alcohol and drank a few bottles before we left her house. I felt very excited; I was escaping into a different world where I didn't think about Mum or her cancer.

By the time we boarded the bus everyone was drunk, including Laura and I. I couldn't believe I was actually sitting on the 'boogie bus'; it felt great to be just like everyone else.

Half an hour later we arrived in Dingwall and everyone clambered off the bus. I could see the neon lights and hear the beat of the music. It was loud and sounded great. I was finally here!

Two very smartly dressed men stood at the entrance to the club. 'Bouncers' I heard someone say. I wasn't sure what they were there for, but Laura and I began to get nervous. What if they didn't let us in?

'Five pounds' they said to everyone in front of us in the queue. When it came to our turn they started laughing 'Evening girls' they said, 'Come back when you are eighteen,' they gave another laugh. My face turned scarlet. I felt so embarrassed. Laura and I walked away as fast as we could, hoping that no one would recognise us.

I turned the corner to see me older sister standing in front of me! 'What on earth are you doing here?' she said, shocked. 'You're kidding me. Did you really believe you would get in?' she asked and burst out laughing. 'Go home,' she ordered and went off laughing with her friends. I couldn't believe she'd seen me. The humiliation! The embarrassment! I knew that she would tell Mum and Dad and the thought of them finding out horrified me.

"I felt that I'd let Mum and Dad down"

I didn't sleep a wink at Laura's. I felt that I'd let Mum and Dad down horribly and I couldn't bear the thought of hurting Mum. I arrived at home the next morning with a long face. I knew that my sister would have told them as this was her moment to get revenge for all the times I had told them about things she'd been doing. I had been the one who had caught her smoking and sneaking off with boys. She now had the perfect opportunity to get even.

As soon as I looked at Mum and I knew that my sister had told her what happened. I began to cry. 'I'm so sorry Mum for letting you down,' I said through my tears. 'I didn't want to hurt you or give you stress.'

Mum sat on the bed and began to laugh. She actually found it quite funny and eventually I joined in. We laughed together for the first time in a very long while. Mum didn't say a word to Dad; she didn't want to cause him any more grief.

I was still determined to get into that night club, no matter what. I wanted to get the better of the bouncers for humiliating me. I chatted about it with Mum. 'Do you think they knew I wasn't eighteen because I'm so small,' I asked her. (I was four foot eight at the time. My sister was only an inch taller.)

'No,' said mum, 'you just looked too young.' Mum said she would help if I really wanted to go. I was amazed and couldn't help wondering if she really meant it. 'I won't get to see you all dressed up when you're eighteen going out and having fun,' she explained. I hated it when she would say these things it really frightened me.

Mum asked my sister to look after me and to stand beside me to make sure that I would get in. This was my sister's worst nightmare; I would be able to watch her and see what she got up to. Dread spread across her face. 'Revenge.' I said to myself.

I saw Laura at school the following Monday 'Plaster on the make-up,' I told her.

'I never want to go there again. The embarrassment was too much,' Laura said, 'I couldn't bear that again. Anyway I need to study for the exams.'

Laura was clever; she didn't need to study very much as she was naturally bright. I knew that Laura liked one of the lads who played in my dad's football team. I also knew that the football team would go out to the pubs and night club on Saturdays after their matches. 'If you go, the lad you like in the football team will be there, I told her. That was all the persuasion she needed.

Saturday night came and once again, I lied to dad. I told him that I was going to do some babysitting.

'Just this once,' said Mum 'I just want to see what you look like all dressed up and share your first experience at a night club. Only drink coke and don't let anyone buy you a drink.' She plastered my face with make-up; eyeliner, lipstick, mascara, the lot, back combed my hair and gave me a pair of my sister's old stilettos. We stuffed the toes with toilet roll so they would fit. We had a great laugh together and I felt so happy. It made a change from all the misery we usually shared.

When I looked at myself in the mirror I didn't look like me; I was staring at someone completely different. Mum was amazed too. 'You will definitely get in, you look beautiful,' she said.

Suddenly there was a bang on the bathroom door; it was dad. Mum and I panicked! He would know for sure that I was not going babysitting if he saw me dressed like this. I pretended I was on the toilet and luckily he went downstairs; I quickly made an exit to my room. 'That was lucky. You had better get out before he catches you.' Mum said quietly.

'Bye dad,' I shouted, 'I'm off to babysit.' Telling lies was becoming part of my new character.

When I met Laura she couldn't believe how I looked. 'You look like a different person, she said, amazed. I liked this different person I had become. When I looked in the mirror I didn't see any sadness or hurt. I could just see a smiling face covered in make-up and I felt it made me look beautiful.

We arrived on the High Street and after a few drinks we boarded the bus. Everyone kept saying how great I looked. I loved all the attention, because it made me feel good about myself. I felt there was no need to worry about anything, and really enjoyed myself. We finally arrived at Dingwall; my stomach was in knots. Could I really pull this off? My hands were sweaty and my heart was racing as we joined the queue.

'Evening ladies. Five pounds please.' I couldn't believe my luck. 'Evening ladies!' I was in; I was finally through those big black doors. For a second I was tempted to say to the bouncers, 'Hey remember me? You wouldn't let me in last week and ha-ha, I'm in now and I'm only fifteen.' Fortunately I managed to keep quiet; otherwise they would have thrown me out as quickly as they had let me in.

The nightclub was like another world. The beat of the music, the lasers and the neon lights, the smell of beer, the feeling of getting drunk, I loved every minute of my time there. I danced all night and it felt like the best night of my life. I didn't want to leave and was disappointed at 1am when it was over and we had to leave, I would have stayed there all night if I could. We boarded the boogie bus to go home. The bus was much quieter than it had been on the way there, as most people were very drunk and others were too busy kissing their boyfriends or someone they had just met. Laura and I had had a great night; we couldn't wait to go again. Mum laughed when I told her about it.

I couldn't think of anything else for the rest of the week. All I wanted to do now was go nightclubbing. I just wanted to tell everyone at school about the best night of my life but no one was interested, they were all too busy worrying about their exams.

Laura had managed to dance with the lad she liked from the football club so she definitely wanted to go back the following week. On Saturday I asked Dad if I could stay at Laura's. That part was the truth; I just didn't mention the night club.

Over the next few Saturday nights I stayed at Laura's and we went to the club together. It was the only thing I had to look forward too; it was my escape.

After many weeks of clubbing, reality finally entered my world of escape: mum began to deteriorate.

A broken heart

I arrived home from school one day and one look at my parents faces told me that there was bad news: the cancer had returned and Mum had to go into hospital for chemotherapy. Mum explained that the chemotherapy would burn the cancer cells in her body.

She also told me that there would be side effects of the treatment, she might get very sick and all her hair would fall out. Both my brother and sister found the news very hard to cope with, especially my brother. He kept all of his feelings bottled inside but I knew he was hurting. As for poor Dad he was so brave and strong but he looked like he had all the worries of the world on his shoulders. I was so angry at what the cancer was doing to my family

"There was bad news"

Mum began her treatment but she didn't take to it very well. After the first session I sat by her bed, watching her vomit and cry, trying to help her in any way that I could. I wiped her head with a face cloth and tried to reassure her that she would be okay. Inside though I had never felt such despair and I couldn't bear it.

Often I would help her to dress and take her to the bathroom as she was becoming more weak and helpless. Some days she was angry and frustrated, others pain and hurt were the overwhelming emotions showing on her face. She began loosing her hair, large clumps falling out in her hairbrush and she decided that she couldn't cope with any more. The side effects of the chemotherapy were too much and she wasn't going to go through any more sessions.

Her life was slowing draining away from her. I begged to be allowed to stay at home and help as I was afraid to leave her side. Eventually she gave in and, with her permission, I stopped going to school.

Although I wasn't going to school I still carried on working at the farm shop in the early evenings. I loved my job as it was something that enabled me to keep going. Word was spreading about Mum's illness but I didn't like to talk about it, I got too upset.

Not long after she had made the decision to stop the chemotherapy, Mum had to go to the hospital to find out what would happen next. I was at work and she promised to call me as soon as she got home to let me know everything was okay.

Every time the phone rang at work my heart raced. I waited all afternoon but no call came and I was beginning to wonder if something was wrong. The shop closed at 5:30. I usually got a lift home with Dad but he wasn't there so I walked home as fast as I could. I dreaded walking in the front door. I was terrified and my stomach was in knots; I knew something was terribly wrong.

I opened the front door and went straight to the sitting room. The house was strangely quiet. Dad stood there white as a sheet, unable to speak. A tear ran down his cheek and he held his arms out to me. My whole body went numb. I knew it was serious, as I had never seen my dad look like this. 'Six weeks is all your mum has left,' he eventually managed to say. He didn't say anything else for the rest of the day.

We had had years and years of preparation for Mum's death but nothing could have prepared me for what I felt right then. I ran upstairs to find Mum in bed. I went straight to her and cuddled her tight. 'Please don't leave me,' I begged her through my tears, 'I don't want you to go. I need you. What will happen to me?' This couldn't be real. Mum just held me tight as our tears overflowed. Our worst nightmare had arrived.

> *"Nothing could have prepared me for what I felt right then."*

I never returned to school and even gave up my job at the farm shop. Every minute of my time was spent by mum's bedside, keeping watch over her. Night after night I would lie awake beside her, unable to sleep. I was terrified that she would die and I would be unable to say goodbye. I stopped eating as I felt sick with worry.

By this time, Mum couldn't speak much. 'Please save your money,' she would say, 'you're going to be on your own. You will have to feed yourself and buy clothes.' It really frightened me when she said these things, especially as Dad would still be around. Mum had always been there for me and always made me feel safe and secure. I started to wonder what would happen to my life when she died?

Mum was getting thinner and thinner; her skin turned yellow. It was heart breaking to see her in so much pain. So much so that, as hard as it would be to lose her I felt it would be better to say goodbye than to watch her suffer any more. The house had become cold and lifeless. No one smiled and hardly a word was spoken.

Eventually Mum's words became fewer and fewer. One day, she asked us all to pray with her. She asked us to tell God that we wouldn't be angry with Him. She said it was time for him to take her home, because her pain was too much for her to bear. We all said her little prayer. Later that night Mum began to cough up blood; her body

"It was heart breaking to see (Mum) in so much pain."

just couldn't take anymore. We held her tight and told her we loved her and she told us she loved us too. The next morning she passed away.

Anger, hurt, and confusion pierced my heart as I looked at Mum's body. I couldn't move; I couldn't speak. For many years Mum had said, 'I'll die one day' and that day had arrived; I would never see her again. My heart was broken.

As I looked at the rest of my family I knew that they were heartbroken too. My brother's response was to scream, shout, kick and punch the wall. I had never seen him like this before; he was always full of love and kindness. The last person I looked at was Dad. His face was colourless; like stone, etched with sorrow, grief and pain. In that moment I lost my whole family; the grief of losing Mum was too much. Our hearts were so broken that we were unable to show any love for each other. The day Mum died I let anger into my heart and shut everyone out.

Dad collapsed at the funeral; he had been living under so much strain for so long that he could take no more. I didn't understand the effect this had on me. I had always been sensitive and cried at the slightest thing but my anger made me cold-hearted and I shed no tears. My whole life had been turned upside down.

Our house became cold and lifeless without Mum at the centre of it. With her love gone the joy and laughter went too along with the sound of the kettle boiling, the rattle of teacups and the smell of home cooked food. Dad was struggling to pay the bills and keep the house going and there was hardly ever any food in the fridge and cupboards.

I returned to my job at the farm shop and decided to try to rekindle the warm homely feeling back in the house. I would go shopping with the little money I made and put all my effort into making Sunday dinner but no one was interested in eating it. Dad and my brother either wouldn't turn up or they would not be hungry. I felt that I had failed.

"Dad was hardly ever around"

Anger and resentment welled up inside me. I felt trapped in the pain and could see no way out. I took my anger out on dad one day. 'How can you say there is a God?' I screamed. I thought of all of my unanswered prayers. There and then I turned my heart from God. To me He didn't exist.

I realised that I was on my own and it was up to me to survive by myself. This was the beginning of a new me, of a new and different life.

Survival

In the weeks following, Dad was hardly ever around. He didn't seem to remember that I existed and I realised the truth of Mum's words; I was on my own. It was down to me to feed and clothe myself.

I returned to school and absolutely hated every minute of it. When I turned up I was rude to the teachers and distracted the other pupils. A lot of the time I didn't bother going at all. Everyone around me put my behaviour down to grief and assumed that I would get over it. They didn't know how I was really feeling; I needed love but didn't know where to look and was unable to find it.

The only thing I looked forward to was hanging out on the High

Street with other kids. One Friday night I was there with my friend Katie and was feeling very down that evening. 'You look sad,' Mark said.

'At last,' I thought, 'someone has actually noticed.' I just longed for someone to care about me. Mark said he had something that would make me feel much better. I didn't care what it was, I just needed something to take the heartache away.

He took out a bag and inside it was a tiny piece of white paper with a strawberry on it. I'd seen these before when the police had come to the school to talk about drugs. They had shown us the tablets and told us they were called LSD or acid. I remembered being told that they were dangerous and could kill, but I didn't care. If I took one and died I would be with Mum again.

I paid Mark a fiver and took one of the tablets. I was frightened but convinced myself that as no one loved me, or even cared about me, I had nothing to lose. The LSD made me laugh hysterically, it was a crazy and completely different experience to being drunk.

I returned home, still very high after taking the drug. Dad was in the front room and I popped my head round the door to say hello. I wanted him to shout and get angry with me for taking drugs, but he didn't even notice. I wondered how he failed to notice that his fifteen year-old daughter was high on drugs? I stormed angrily up to bed. The dad I knew would have noticed my drugged state immediately but since Mum had died he had become lost in his own world of sorrow. After that night I decided that Dad didn't care about me.

As no one cared what I did, I decided to try smoking. Within weeks of my mum's death I had gone from being a reasonably good kid to one who was drinking, smoking and taking LSD on a regular basis.

"No one took any interest in what I was doing"

I was living a secret life. No one in my family knew what I was doing because they were too lost in their grief. I had recently started catering college but I had no interest in it and no one took any interest in what I was doing so I wondered why I was bothering. I had also restarted my job at the farm shop and that was what that kept me going. I worked hard all week and my wages provided enough for me to live on and to pay for my drinking and drugs habit. I started to live for the weekends. I had become a big part of the in crowd and was known by everyone in the village.

My confidence grew and I decided to chance my luck and see if I would be served in the pub. I plastered my face in make up to make myself appear older. I was served the first time I tried it, and from there had the courage to try them all. My group of friends grew bigger and became more well known, especially for our love of drink. I would drink huge quantities every weekend, in various pubs around the area and walk home through the estate singing my favourite Dolly Parton song 'Working Nine to Five' at the top of my voice. I felt that the song was me; I had left college and now worked six days a week, earning a lot more money. That suited me as the more money I had, the more I was able to spend on drugs and alcohol.

I soon started to smoke hash and weed, mixing it with the alcohol. I would take 'whities' and pass out. I would often end the evening vomiting in the street; drinking was beginning to overtake me. I realised that it wasn't that I enjoyed drinking, it had become my way of comforting my broken heart.

People had started to talk about me; I didn't want to lose my good reputation.

My working life wasn't going so well either. The farm shop had been losing sales because a new supermarket had opened in the High Street and there were rumours that it was closing down. I was worried when I heard them as I loved my job. It was my life, it was also my only means of providing food and clothing. I liked designer clothes and always kept up with the latest fashion trends. With no job I really would have nothing. I knew I would find it difficult to get another job, as I had no qualifications having not bothered with school and dropped out of college. Dad barely made ends meet and I knew that I couldn't depend on him.

One night I received an unexpected phone call from Jane, a girl who used to live in Invergordon but had moved to London after her dad had died. 'I'm ringing to find out if you're interested in coming to London,' she said, 'there is a nanny job available.' I told her I would think about it and call her back.

I lay in bed that night and thought about London. I wondered if it was my only option for survival. I'd only ever known the Highlands and London seemed very far away and very scary. I phoned Jane the following day and told her that I wasn't sure about the job.

'You will have your own room and bathroom,' she said 'and in September you will be going to America. If you come to work for us we will bring you with us to America.' I used to watch programmes about America on the television. Going there would be a dream come true!

I looked around me; the house had no life left in it and the kitchen had fallen apart. I was too embarrassed to invite friends home. I told Jane that I would go to London for the interview. London would mean a new home, a new life and a new beginning.

Lost

The following week I travelled to Inverness and boarded the coach to London. I had mixed feelings about the trip; Scotland was my home, it was a safe, friendly, warm and loving place and I didn't want to leave. I did however feel that I didn't have much choice.

Twelve hours later I arrived at Victoria coach station. I stepped off the coach and the sights and sounds of London overwhelmed me. There were so many people of different colours, all rushing about.

'You must be Kelly?' I heard a voice behind me. 'Don't worry I'll look after you.' The lady's name was Nita and I would be working for her if I got the job. Her house was in North London and we drove through London, passing by Buckingham Palace. Everything I saw seemed so big and the buildings were beautiful.

"I could not bear the thought of being rejected again."

As we pulled up outside Nita's house in Golders Green, I suddenly felt afraid: suppose her family didn't like me. I could not bear the thought of being rejected again.

Compared to our little council house in Invergordon, Nita's house looked like a palace. I could smell sausages cooking as we walked in, it felt so homely and full of life. The first person I was introduced to was Samaria, the little girl I would be looking after. They were celebrating her birthday and a party was in full swing with caterers, entertainers and lots of guests. It amazed me how these people lived; I had never seen so much food. Everyone seemed so kind and friendly and I started to wonder if this could compensate for the family home I had lost.

I fell in love with Samaria straight away. I thought that I had forgotten how to love, but this little girl managed to make a small place in my heart. I knew if I got the job it would be easy to love her and take care of her. However, I still had mixed feelings about whether I would be able to leave my life in Scotland.

Jane popped in to see me and the family told us to go out for a few hours and see some of London. As we walked along the road, I noticed that, although it was evening the area was full of life. It was such a busy place with plenty of restaurants, bars, and a night club. It was so different to Invergordon where all the shops closed at six o'clock. I was fascinated by it but still unsure about whether it was the right place for me.

My interview with the family was the following morning but I had nothing to do for the rest of the day. When Jane came over and asked if I would like to go to a place called Camden Town I jumped at the chance to see more of London. As we walked to the underground station, I was intrigued by number of the different looking people I saw; including a group of people with long curly hair and big hats. Jane explained that they were Jews. I had only heard about Jews once in Sunday School but had never seen them in real life before; I hadn't even realised that they weren't just characters in the Bible and I realised how sheltered my life in Scotland had been.

The underground station was dark, smelly and unpleasant. We arrived at Camden Town, got off the train and headed up the escalator. As I walked out the underground station I froze and was unable to move for about five minutes. It felt like I had entered a completely different world. Punk rockers, Goths, people with crazy hair and outrageous clothes. My first thought was, 'I could get lost here.' I didn't mean physically lost, I meant lost in this world of being who I wanted to be and doing what I liked.

You couldn't hide in Invergordon; there was always someone talking about what you wore, what you had and what you looked like. The thought of escaping from that and being invisible appealed. I craved a life of freedom; to be who I wanted to, dress how I wanted to and not worry about what anybody else thought. Jane promised that she would look after me if I decided to move to London. She asked how I liked Camden Town and I responded that I loved it. She was visibly shocked and told me that she'd only taken me there to scare me, to see if it would put me off leaving the Highlands. It hadn't. We returned to Nita's and I went to bed

In the last few weeks, old friends of my mum had been stopping me on the High Street, 'It's a disgrace what's happened to your family,' they would say. 'Your father should be looking after you. You're out getting drunk every week. Your Mum would be horrified.' I was sick and tired of hearing it and wondered if leaving would be the best thing for me.

I left the following morning and Nita said that she'd call during the week to let me know if I had been successful. I had lots to think about on the coach on the way home. Before Mum had died I would never have imagined myself in London but I found myself very tempted.

When I arrived home, the village seemed so lifeless. I shared my experiences of London with my dad and then went next door to talk to our neighbour who had been Mum's friend for a long time.

'I have some bad news,' she said. 'I have seen your father with another woman.' Anger ripped through my whole body and I wondered how he could betray Mum like that. I knew if I saw my dad with another woman we would argue as no one could ever replace Mum in my mind and I didn't know why he didn't feel the same way. This news helped me to make up my mind about going to London as I knew that I would never be able to accept another woman in Mum's place. I realise now that it was unfair to expect dad to live the rest of his life alone; he needed someone to love him, but at that time I was so full of hurt and pain I couldn't understand how he could move on so quickly.

I spoke to my dad later and mentioned that my neighbour had told me he was seeing another woman. We had a huge fight; I had never screamed and shouted at Dad before and I knew I had really upset him.

I told him that if he dared to bring a woman into the house I would leave.

The day after I arrived home I had a phone call from Nita to say that the job was mine if I wanted it. I still wasn't ready to make a final decision but I said 'yes' immediately, knowing that the start date was six weeks later and I would have time to change my mind.

I decided to tell Dad first as I wanted to see what he would say. I felt sure that if he really loved me he wouldn't allow me to go to London and if he said it was a bad idea I would stay. 'That's great.' He said and once again my blood boiled. I felt rejected by him. Was the dad who moved us away from Glasgow as he didn't want us to grow up there really going to allow me to move to London? I didn't understand how he could bear to let me go to such a big city on my own where anything could happen. At that point I convinced myself that Dad didn't love me and couldn't wait for me to leave.

I started to tell other people in the village that I would be moving to London. They told me that it was a great thing and how I was going to be able to make something of my life. I enjoyed the way they had started to look up to me but deep down inside I was petrified. I just wanted a normal life with a mum, dad and a loving home but that was no longer a possibility.

"Deep down inside I was petrified."

The weeks before I was due to leave passed by quickly. I spent my last night in Scotland curled up on my bed crying. I was sure that if Dad saw how swollen my eyes were, he would know that I'd been crying and realise that I didn't want to leave. I was still in tears when he arrived home from his night shift, earlier than usual, so that he could take me to Inverness to catch the train.

'Are you ready to go?' he said. I couldn't believe that he hadn't noticed my tears or that he didn't understand what they meant.

I cried all the way to Inverness. I longed for Dad to tell me to stay, to hear him say the words 'Don't go' but he didn't say a word. 'Please Dad, please' I kept saying in my head, 'just say those words.'

Tears were running down my cheeks as I boarded the train and I was screaming inside 'Please, if you love me just tell me to get off the train and come home. Forget all about London and everything will be okay.'

The only thing he did say was 'You will be okay.' As I looked into his face it was cold and hard, just as it had been since the day Mum had died. My brother looked the same, and once again my heart broke as I said 'Goodbye' to those I loved but was unable to reach out to. A suitcase and £80 was all I had in the world. Mum's words ran through my head and I knew that she'd been right. I was on my own and had to look after myself now.

"I was on my own and had to look after myself now."

31

Part Two

No one was there to meet me when I finally arrived at Kings Cross station. Nita had told me to get a black cab from the station and I felt lost and alone as I tried to navigate the station. I wasn't used to being around so many different people, from so many different backgrounds. I had grown up in a small village where I knew everyone, now the only person I knew in London was Jane.

"I felt lost and alone"

From the age of fifteen I had been frequenting nightclubs, getting drunk and taking drugs but I had never been as frightened as I was statnding on my own at Kings Cross. I managed to find a black cab, which was a terrifying experience as I'd never been in a taxi on my own before. Even though I no longer believed God existed, I prayed all the way to Nita's house in Golders Green 'Please God just get me there safely.'

Nita's house didn't feel the same as it had when I'd visited for my interview. There was no smell of home cooked food and the house was very quiet. Nita showed me to my room and I lay on my bed feeling incredibly lonely.

Nita warned me that Jane had been drinking a lot and she didn't want me to do that. I didn't want to drink. I knew that this was my new home and I couldn't afford to lose it.

The following day was Sunday and Jane came to see me. We decided to go out for a while, as Jane wanted to take me to the local pub. I thought it was great that the pubs were open as they still closed on Sundays in Invergordon. Jane introduced me to a few of the regulars who were from Scotland. Having something in common, I warmed to them straight away. They were a lot rougher than the friends I had in Scotland, but they seemed okay.

I started work on Monday and was expected to work from 7am to 7pm. Samaria's grandparents arrived to show me around Golders Green so that I could get used to going out on my own. The next day I was on my own. Samaria and I walked to the High Street and I was shocked to see that everyone looked so stern and unhappy. I was used to a town full of jolly people, smiling faces and a friendly atmosphere. We popped into a Seven-Eleven and a man pushed into me. I told him that he was rude and should apologise but he just looked at me as if I was a piece of rubbish. 'You're rude!' I shouted as he left the shop.

I realised that life in the city was going to be very different and would take some getting used to. I was missing Invergordon already.

It was my intention not to drink, but Jane arrived as soon as I finished work and she took me to the pub. I wasn't sure what else to do with my spare time and found myself in the pub every night after work. Jane and I both looked forward to having a drink as we felt we needed it after a long and busy day. I earned £80, which didn't seem much compared to the £230 I'd earned in Scotland but I had no rent to pay or food to buy. My wages were just enough to buy a drink every night and to get really drunk at the weekend.

I started to live for Friday nights. The pubs and clubs were really busy and I could go wild, as I didn't have to work the following day. Sometimes we would go to Leicester Square, Covert Garden, Soho, Kings Cross or Victoria. Leicester Square was always full of interesting people and I loved to sit and talk to the drag queens, as I'd never seen anyone like them before. In Soho I would watch the prostitutes. To me, London was the University of Life. I felt that I'd lived such a sheltered life, and couldn't imagine drag queens, prostitutes or gay night clubs in the Highlands of Scotland. I started to wonder if this was what life was all about.

"London was the University of Life"

At Christmas I had been in London for five months and Nita bought me a ticket to Scotland so that I could do home. I was so excited as I couldn't wait to see my old friends and tell them about my life in London.

I arrived home to find that another woman had moved into the house. I was so angry with Dad and wished that I'd not gone home. Jane had also gone home for the holiday and arrived in my house in tears as her mum's boyfriend had hit her. Jane and I spent every night getting drunk until we were able to return to London.

Back in London, we started drinking more. Both of us tried to put on a brave face but the trip to Scotland had been too much for us to take. Jane was heartbroken about what had happened in her family and I felt betrayed by mine.

Jane and I had gotten to know the manager at the local bar and nightclub and asked if they had any jobs available. We worked in the bar at the weekend and they paid us in alcohol. This meant that we were able to drink throughout the week for free. I didn't tell Nita about my second job as I knew that she would fire me if she knew what I was doing every evening.

I loved working in the nightclub and began to find working as a nanny very boring. Keeping on top of two jobs was hard work and I don't know how I managed to pull it off. Some nights I would still be in the nightclub until 6am and have to plaster my face with make up to avoid looking hung-over.

Different men would ask us out every week. I was used to being on my own and had been doing what I liked since I was fifteen. Although I enjoyed chatting and flirting I wanted to keep my options open, as I didn't want to get tied down to one boyfriend.

I got used to the regulars at the club but would always be wary of unfamiliar faces. A new crowd of men began to appear every Friday and they would always ask Jane and I to sit with them and drink champagne. I was always reluctant as there was something about them that I didn't trust. One of them kept asking me out and I would always refuse. In the end, the bouncers had a word with him and asked him to stop bothering me. He ignored them and they eventually made them leave and warned them not to come back.

A week later, the club was closed and as usual, Jane and I were sitting with the bouncers and managers having a drink. At about three o'clock in the morning we heard a loud bang on the door. The bouncers thought it might be the police so they went to check, but as they opened the door a crowd of men came rushing in. One of them hit the bouncer over the head with an iron bar. I ran for my life as I'd recognised two of the men from the previous week and I'd never been so petrified in my life. Jane ran one way and I hid in the cupboard.

"I ran for my life"

The men ransacked the whole club. I heard screaming and shouting as they smashed the bar to pieces before bringing out knives and machetes. There was blood everywhere when they finished; the bouncers were in a terrible way, all bashed and beaten.

At last they left but we were afraid to go outside in case any of the gang were still hanging around. At around 5:30am we thought it would be safe and Jane and I both needed to be at work by seven o'clock. The bouncers checked outside and it seemed to be safe for us to leave. It was only ten minutes walk to our house but it felt like forever, Jane and I held on to each other for dear life. We couldn't stop shaking and we jumped at the slightest sound.

After that night we gave up working in the nightclub. We didn't ever want to go through that experience again. I liked excitement but this was too much.

My drinking was getting worse and I needed more money, as I was no longer getting free drinks. Nita had fallen pregnant and she told me I needed learn to drive in order to help her out more. I told her that I couldn't afford lessons so she said she would pay and handed me a check for £200. It had been a long time since I had had so much money. I had a few lessons then Jane and I spent the rest of the money on alcohol. I lied to Nita and thought that I would get away with it.

I had grown to hate working for Nita. I was sure that the family looked down on me and I felt like a slave, but I had no other choice but to continue working there, as they provided the roof over my head.

Jane announced she was leaving London to go to work in Belgium. My heart sank and I felt angry with her; she had promised she would look after me. She said that she was sorry but she had to go. Her drinking was getting out of control and she wanted to go away and sort herself out. I thought that I should sort myself out too as I needed to stop drinking so much. My work was getting slack and Nita had found out that I had lied about the driving lessons.

Jane had only been gone a week when Nita landed a bombshell on me 'I am giving you three weeks' notice, you will have to go.' My whole world collapsed at her words. I didn't know where I was to go, or what I would do. I was now frightened for my life and I had no one to turn to.

I needed to sober up quickly and work out what I was going to do. I was going to be homeless, as I couldn't even afford a deposit for a room.

My only option was to ring Dad. I called home and my brother answered the phone. He told me he wasn't happy and was moving out. He said Dad had a girlfriend who didn't want him round. My Dad had always really loved my brother; I knew that if he didn't want him around he definitely wouldn't want me around.

When I arrived in London I was dressed in the latest fashions, but I had really let myself go. Every penny I had earned had been spent on alcohol, clubs and drugs. I had really messed things up and I realised I had no choice but to ring Dad again. I told him that I had no job and nowhere to go. 'Come home if you want to,' he said, 'but I'm sure you will be okay in London'.

"I had really let myself go" I didn't feel convinced that he really wanted me to go home, as there was no concern in his voice. I wanted him to make a fuss and tell me that my only option was to come home but his voice didn't reassure me at all. It was as if he didn't want me there; he knew that I would only get in the way and cause arguments if he had a woman in the house.

I stormed out of the house and went immediately to the pub to drown my sorrows. My time was running out; I only had a week left at Nita's. I applied for a job as a nanny that was advertised in the local paper and went for the interview. In the meantime I found myself a few cleaning jobs. Cleaning people's dirty toilets and scrubbing ovens was not how I imagined life in London would to turn out to be, but I was grateful for the work and money.

I really needed the job that I had been interviewed for. I returned to Nita's and lay on my bed. Once again I called out to God with all my heart: 'Please God I really need that job.' Later that week I received a phone call to say that I had got the job. It was a live out job so my biggest problem now was finding somewhere to live. I walked down Golders Green High Street thinking about what I would do. I had seen so many homeless people in the West End, sleeping in shop doorways in their sleeping bag and I thought this would be my only option. I looked in the back alleys and shop doorways, wondering which would be safer for me to sleep in and came to the conclusion that the back alley would be slightly safer. I had enough money to buy myself a sleeping bag. No one would know I was there.

Oh how I wished that Mum was still alive. I had really made a mess of my life. I was petrified that I would be found dead in a back alley and wondered if anyone would even miss me. I told myself that if I stayed in the pub until closing time, I would have drunk enough to keep myself warm throughout the night and it wouldn't bother me.

I was due to start my new job in a few weeks and planned to rent a room as soon as I'd saved enough money for a deposit. It was definitely not the life I had wanted or imagined but I felt that I had no choice and would have to sleep on the streets until I got myself sorted out. Other people survived, I would too.

No one ever saw me without make up on but I had cried so much walking along Golders Green High Street that I'd washed it all away by the time I arrived at the pub. I knew that I looked dreadful but I didn't care anymore. I ordered a drink and sat down on my own.

A dirty, sleazy looking man approached me; his fingers were stained with nicotine, his beard had turned yellow and his clothes were filthy. 'I'm Harry' he introduced himself. 'You're Kelly,' he said, 'I've watched you come in here all year.' I gave him a false smile and hoped that he'd go away and leave me alone. 'You look dreadful,' he continued. 'You look like it's the end of the world. Are you okay?'

I began to soften towards him, as he was the first person who had shown any kindness towards me. I told him how I had lost my job and was homeless. He said he might be able to help. I was grateful but couldn't help wondering if he really wanted to help or if he was taking advantage of me?

Harry lived in a house that he shared with a group of regulars at the pub. I knew them well and they were very fond of me. A guy called Sam lived in one of the rooms but he was rarely there and Harry said I could have his room until I sorted myself out. The rent was £50 a week but at least I didn't have to sleep on the street.

I was very grateful to Harry. I gave him a big hug (despite his filthy clothes). The room was only a temporary place and I could get thrown out at any time. I told myself I would really have to give up drinking this time, but still arranged to meet Harry at the pub on Friday.

It was my last day at Nita's. I lay on my bed and remembered some of my experiences in that house: the night's I would sneak Jane into my room to sleep, and the boys from Scotland we would sometimes sneak in too.

One night I got so drunk that I couldn't even see my key on the key ring. As I couldn't get in the front door, I had to climb over the ten foot wall that had broken glass bottles concreted onto the top of it. The broken glass ripped my legs and arms, but I knew that I had to get over. I turned and cut the side of my face as I slid down the other side of the wall. Luckily I didn't feel the pain very much as I was so drunk. I managed to get a few hours sleep but realised how much of a mess I was in when I woke. I was cut, sore and very hung over.

At the weekend, I would often start the day with a drink. I felt very let down by Nita, she had promised me great things including a trip to America but nothing had ever materialised.

Despite this, I loved Samaria. We had some lovely times together during the time I looked after her. We would stroll through the park, eat ice cream in the pavilion, feed the ducks, and go to see the animals at the zoo. When I finished work Samaria would often sit outside my door crying and screaming for me to let her in. I wanted to but her mother would not allow it; she wanted her daughter to love her rather than me. Week after week, I watched as they spent hundreds of pounds on designer clothes and toys for Samaria but what she needed from them was love. I hoped she would have someone to love her as much as I did.

Nita arrived home from work. 'Are you ready to go?' she asked. 'Make sure you have everything.' Her face was cold and hard. 'Say goodbye to Kelly, Samaria.'

I told Samaria that I loved her and would never forget her and I meant it. After mum died I had been unable to love anyone but I had grown to love that little girl and I hoped that she would soon have someone who loved her as much as I did.

Nita handed me my weekly wage of £80, walked to the door and said goodbye. My anger towards her was raging inside. She didn't offer me a lift or care where I was going. I felt that she had used me and when she was finished with me she had just got rid of me. I wondered how she could be so cruel and heartless. The door slammed behind me. 'Don't cry,' I said to myself. I had to be tough.

As I walked down the cobbled street, dragging my suitcase behind me, I felt rejected and alone. I was hurt and angry. Angry with Mum for dying, angry with Dad for not giving me the love that I needed, angry with Nita and angry with life in general. I longed for my family but they were beyond my reach. I just wanted my life to be over, I felt like giving up.

I arrived at the pub and told myself to 'Put on a brave face.' Harry was there and seemed delighted to see me. He looked so dirty and sleazy that my stomach turned. This was all I had to help me. I knew that I was taking a risk and was almost tempted to walk out and find a dark alley to sleep in. I couldn't be sure that he wasn't lying to me. He could get me back to his place and do anything. I felt so afraid but didn't have many options open to me so I had a few drinks to calm me down and then we left.

It was cold and dark as we walked to the bus stop. I was so nervous that my stomach was turning and I prayed I would be okay. As we got on the bus I realised that I didn't know anything about Harry, where the house was, or even if it existed. I didn't want him to sense that he frightened me, so I tried to keep a brave face and act tough. The house was a five minute walk from the bus stop and we soon arrived there. The house existed, 'Thank God,' I said to myself.

"I tried to keep a brave face and act tough."

The house was damp, cold and smelly. Light bulbs hung down from the ceiling with no lampshades. In the kitchen, dirty dishes were piled up in the sink and mould was growing all over the windows. The net curtains were black with dirt. There was an old green sofa in the front room along with an old fashioned television and video recorder. This was so different to the house lived in for the past year but I was just grateful to have a roof over my head.

'Remember your rent every Friday,' Harry said 'or there will be trouble.' I assured him that he would get his money. I would make sure that I paid the rent, even if I had to scrub more dirty toilets. I thanked Harry for letting me stay.

He showed me to a room at the top of the stairs. I was relieved to see that the door had a lock. There was also an old bed and wardrobe. I lay down on the bed and sighed with relief. It could have been much worse. I curled up, pulled the old smelly blanket over me and tried to sleep. I was now completely on my own; this was my life.

I got up early the next morning and headed to the market to buy a duvet and some cleaning equipment. I went home and cleaned the whole house. It looked and smelled so much cleaner and I was pleased with how much I'd achieved. Harry was delighted when he came home.

I invited Sophie, a friend of mine to visit my new home. She was horrified. 'It's disgusting!' she said. 'Are you really going to live here?' I felt ashamed and embarrassed. When I was working for Nita we had lived on the richest road in Golders Green. Sophie didn't understand that this was my life and I had no choice. She had family in London and they obviously loved her. She didn't visit the house again.

"Money was very tight"

Money was very tight and I continued with the cleaning jobs until I started my new job as a nanny. I only earned enough to pay for rent, gas, electricity and a small amount of food. I just got on with it, I felt as if I was no good and allowed people to treat me badly.

I spent all of my spare time in the pub and it began to feel like home, as there was always someone there to talk to. I was becoming one of the regulars and I started to trust some of the other regulars, many of whom were Scottish. People could tell that I was vulnerable and would take advantage of me by lying and stealing. My heart became harder each time this happened.

I soon learned that Harry was an alcoholic and a drug addict. Alcohol had cost him his wife and children; he'd loved them but the drink had taken over his life. I saw that despite his hardened face, his heart was broken. Many of the pub regulars had similar stories to Harry and me: broken homes, broken marriages, abuse and death. I felt comfortable with them as their lives were as much of a mess as mine was. We put on brave faces but inside our hearts were broken.

The guys in the pub became like brothers to me. I was only 4ft 10 and some of them were over six feet tall. I felt safe with them; they would stand up for me if any man annoyed me.

I started my new job. It was hard work, I was up at six o'clock every morning, but the family were nice and treated me with kindness and respect. I knew that I couldn't afford to lose my job and ensured that I was polite, kind, loving and caring whilst at work. The family praised me highly for the way that I disciplined the children and I was thankful that my parents had taught me right from wrong.

As soon as I finished work I became a different person. The nice, polite girl I had been, and still was during my working hours, disappeared. I had become rough; I would shout and swear and was always ready to fight if there was the opportunity. It was as if there were two different people living inside of me.

"I had become rough"

I became friends with a girl called Natalie, who was a nanny too. We were very similar and both lived for the weekend. When her employers asked her to leave as they'd caught her with a man in her bedroom, Harry offered her the room next to mine, as it was vacant. She had no deposit for a room, so took Harry up on his offer even though she didn't like him. I enjoyed having another girl in the house as it made me feel safer.

I was in the club one night when a man asked me to dance. I had a bad feeling about him so turned my back and ignored him. As we left he asked me why I didn't want to dance with him. 'I just didn't,' I said, 'no reason,' He became very angry and offensive. Something about him disturbed me but my gang told him to leave and fortunately he never appeared at the club again.

I now had a regular weekend routine: drink, smoke a spiff and get outrageously drunk. Natalie came from Kilburn and she kept begging me to go with her to some of the Irish clubs and pubs in that part of town. I didn't want to get sucked into her way of life but I was starting to get bored in Golders Green. Eventually I gave in and went with her. I was full of energy and, being new, everyone wanted to get to know me. Natalie and I had a reputation for being the terrible two. We drank just like men; in fact we would often drink more than men. I found the attention exciting and people wanted to be around me as they knew that I'd do anything for a laugh. I soon became part of the Kilburn crowd.

As the weeks went by I found that I was being drawn into a different world. Some Saturdays Natalie and I would end up so drunk that we would wake up in bed in the houses of people we didn't know. We would also bring different men home and party all night.

Harry wasn't pleased about the parties as he didn't like different men coming and going. I didn't want to get on the wrong side of him, so I made sure I paid the rent every Friday.

A few of the regulars from the pub were bouncers at the nightclub in Kilburn which had the reputation of being the best club in the area. I knew that one of the bouncers liked me and I would flirt with him and pretend that I liked him so that I could get into the club for free. Being friends with them was great as champagne, vodka and drugs would flow freely when they were around and we would always stay after the club closed; I felt special because I was living a lifestyle that I loved but couldn't afford, for free.

It all ended abruptly one night when a drug deal went wrong and one of the bouncers was killed. The club closed after that and the atmosphere in Kilburn changed. That was the end of my excitement.

I was starting to get bored with Kilburn and slowly drifted back to Golders Green. A few friends were going on holiday and I desperately wanted to go with them but there was no way that I could afford it. I had never been on holiday as a child and longed to go abroad.

A few of the regulars at the pub in Golders Green were fraudsters. They knew all about banks and credit cards and told me how to scam the bank. I got a credit card and cheque book, it was so easy and I had a great time using my new credit card; I ate in nice restaurants, bought new clothes and booked a holiday to Spain. I knew I wouldn't be able to pay the money back but I didn't care. For once I was going to enjoy myself and face the consequences later. I also used stolen credit cards to buy cigarettes and alcohol. I felt bad to start with, but as no one else cared, neither did I.

"I was going to enjoy myself and face the consequences later."

Harry's behaviour towards us was getting out of hand. He would come home in the early hours of the morning and try to force his way into my room, when I didn't respond he would kick the door and scream to be let in. I pretended that I was asleep, and if I ignored him for long enough he would leave.

I'd heard rumours that he owed money to some drug dealers and they were after him. Some heavies came to the pub and threatened to do Harry over if he didn't pay them the money he owed. Harry told us to tell anyone who came to the house that he didn't live there anymore.

One night I arrived home and noticed that the video recorder was missing. I was surprised but wondered if Harry or Max, another tenant, had taken it to be fixed. I needed an early night so I locked the door, climbed into bed and snuggled under the blanket. A few minutes later I was startled by what sounded like footsteps in the bathroom. I heard it again and froze: someone was in the house. I was terrified. Normally if one of us came into the house we would shout to see if anyone else was home so I knew it wasn't one of my housemates. The handle of my door began to turn which petrified me. If they knew I was there they might smash my door in and rape or murder me. Unable to do anything else, I prayed: 'Please God, don't let anyone harm me!' I was frozen with fear. I heard the intruder try all of the other door handles; they were locked.

I heard the footsteps go downstairs, and then I heard smashing and banging. It got louder and louder and I realised that they were smashing up the entire ground floor. I took my blanket and, as quietly as I could, I hid in a cupboard in my room. It seemed like the noise wouldn't stop. The dog next door was barking very loudly and I felt sure that the neighbours would hear and call the police but they didn't. After half an hour the noise stopped. I listened to be sure they had gone but I was too scared to move.

At about two in the morning, I was startled by a loud bang on the door. It was Natalie shouting for me to open the door. Still frightened, I went downstairs to open the door. The person who had been in the house had put the catch on the inside, which was why she couldn't get in. 'You're as white as a ghost,' she said, 'what's happened?

I looked around and saw that Harry's door had been smashed to pieces. Just as we were about to call the police, a car pulled up. Harry and Max were home. Harry went mad and Max said not to call the police; he would deal with it. Another car pulled up outside the house and two men got out. My heart jumped: I was sure that the men had come back. Max grabbed a weapon, charged out the house and chased them down the road. Natalie screamed at him to stop as it was just two men she had invited back from the pub.

I returned to my room and got a shock: my whole bed was covered in wasps. I realised that the intruders must have disturbed a nest. It was turning into an awful night. Natalie's friend Stephen helped clean them up with a vacuum cleaner but I was afraid to get into bed. Stephen kindly stayed in my room.

None of us left the house the next day in case anyone was watching. Max eventually sorted everything out for Harry and his debt was paid. He assured us that the men wouldn't come back.

I had hoped that things would start to improve, but Harry got worse. He would get drunk and find any excuse to lose his temper and break things in the house. We often had no gas or electricity that winter as Harry refused to give us cards for the meters; the house was freezing. Eventually the owner of the house asked Harry to leave, he refused and had to be taken to court.

The owner of the house was a kind man. He owned lots of properties in London and offered Natalie and I a new one-bedroom flat in Cricklewood. We leapt at the chance of having our own place. I had the bedroom and we turned the living room into Natalie's bedroom, as the kitchen was big enough to fit a sofa in. The flat was small but it was nice and clean. Best of all, we didn't have to deal with Harry which meant that I could now rest easily at night. I was happy to be in my new home.

Cricklewood was very different from Golders Green. It had a dark atmosphere and the people seemed rougher and angrier. I knew that I had to make the most of it. There was little chance that I would ever go back to Scotland. There was no reason for me to return, especially as my relationship with Dad hadn't improved.

One evening I was waiting at a bus stop at North Finchley, on my way home from work. As the bus pulled up I looked to my side and saw the man I had refused to dance with at the club. I got on the bus and sat down. He looked angrily at me and sat down next to me. 'Remember me?' he said.

'How could I forget,' I thought to myself, but outwardly I pretended not to remember him.

'Why wouldn't you dance with me?' he asked. He started to call me names and get aggressive. 'When the bus stops in Finchley Central, I'm going to drag you off and sort you out. I'm going to bring you to my flat and do things to you no one has done before. You racist bitch!' he sneered at me.

Race had had nothing to do with it. I often told blokes that I didn't want to dance and didn't understand what his problem was. He continued to say nasty things to me. All sorts of thoughts raced through my mind and I called out to God again: 'Please send me help!'

"I called out to God again"

The bus stopped and a man got on who I saw on my way to work every morning. 'Can I sit next to you?' I asked him, 'this guy is hassling me.'

'Sure,' he said. I got up and the nasty bloke said nothing. I explained to the man what he was trying to do.

'Don't worry, I'll make sure you're okay,' he said. The bus pulled up at Golders Green, right outside the wine bar I always went to. 'Will you be okay?' he asked. The man seemed like an angel sent from God and I knew I'd be fine.

I got off the bus and went into the wine bar, the man threatening me got off too and followed me in. I saw my friend Andrew, and I told him what happened. Within seconds a few of the guys took the man out the back and warned him that if he ever so much as opened his mouth or looked at me again they would break his legs.

Everything was starting to get on top of me. Living in London on my own was difficult and I always worried about paying the rent on my flat. I also felt that my drinking was still out of control. I met another nanny called Hannah and we would meet up during the day so that the children could play together. 'Do you believe in God?' Hannah said to me one day.

'No', I replied.

'I do.' she said.

She asked why I didn't believe and I told her that I was angry with God for taking my mum away and destroying my life. 'But,' I said to

Hannah, 'I find it funny that many times when I am really scared or in desperate situation I've prayed and I have been okay.'

'God hears your prayers and answers them,' she said.

'How do you know it's not just coincidence? I asked.

'No,' she said. 'God is real and Jesus Christ is alive. Come to church with me on Sunday you will love it.

'Maybe one day,' I said.

Hannah had just moved to London and didn't know many people. I felt sorry for her and invited her to my flat one Friday. I stopped at the wine bar on my way home, half regretting inviting her over as I didn't really want to go home after only one drink but I also didn't want to let Hannah down.

As I sat at the bar as usual, Andrew came in and said, 'I'm going to a party tonight. I'd love you to come.' I was surprised; Andrew was Scottish so I trusted him and good looking so I was quite flattered. I really wanted to go with him to the party but I said I couldn't because a friend was coming over.

'Bring her too,' he said. 'I'll pick you up at nine. Ring me when you get home.'

Hannah was so straight-laced that I didn't think she would agree to come to the party but she did. The party was in huge house. There was an overpowering smell of weed as soon as we entered and I felt embarrassed being with Hannah because she looked so boring. Andrew and I laughed at her when we discovered that she'd never had alcohol or been at a party like this before. Champagne, weed, *"I longed to feel loved"* heroin and cocaine flowed. Andrew introduced me to everyone, including all of the big drug dealers. I longed to feel loved and they made me feel special. It was only later that I realised that they didn't love me or care about me; they only wanted me for sex.

That night at the party I got high, so did Hannah. I don't even remember leaving the party and getting home but I woke up in bed with Andrew beside me. I instantly realised that he had taken me to the party to get me high so that he could take advantage of me. I had tried to keep hold of my virginity because of the promise that I had made to my mum. I had trusted Andrew. I didn't think he would treat me in that way and he had betrayed my trust. I felt so cheated that night.

This is what happens in London and other big cities and so many men had tried to do this to me before. Men see vulnerable girls, they take them out and give them drugs and alcohol, they make them feel special and pretend to love them. All they want is to use them for sex.

I rang Hannah to find out if she was okay and asked if I could come and see her. She said she had been sick; I think someone spiked her drink.

'I'm sorry.' I said, 'I'll never take you to one of those parties again.' She was a good person and I felt so bad.

'Please come to church on Sunday,' she said.

'Church,' I said, 'you must be joking!' Church that was the last thing I needed now. I had entered another world of drugs, champagne and parties with some of the biggest drug dealers around who showed me love. I wasn't going to say no to having fun.

'Please Kelly', she begged, 'that life is no good. You will end up in a big mess. Those drugs will kill you. Those people don't love you; they just want to use you.'

I was cross for the first time in ages. Who did she think that she was, telling me what to do? 'This is my life', I said, 'you go and have your church. It's my life and I'll do what I want'.

I was angry with Hannah and tried to avoid her. I didn't return her calls and would pretend to be out if she came to the flat. She sent me a message saying that she knew I was avoiding her. 'I'll pray for you that you go to church one day.' She said. I never saw her again after that.

"I started drinking more heavily."

Deep down, underneath all of my anger I did feel that there was a God but I couldn't be sure. I knew that in my most difficult times I would always say a little prayer. The God thing was confusing to me though and I didn't want to think about it.

I started drinking more heavily. I was always loud and daring, always up for a laugh or joke. No one knew what was really going on inside me, behind all my layers of make-up.

I soon realised that Hannah's words were true; my life was becoming a bigger mess. I was spending time with some of the biggest drug dealers in London and they had started to offer me a lot of money go abroad and smuggle drugs into the country.

My life was spent scrimping and saving to try and make ends meet and I was very tempted. I was taken to private locations where meetings had been arranged but I couldn't go through with it. The thought of being sent to prison for the next ten years was too terrifying.

I felt like a fool for falling for their lies. I realised that I wasn't special to them; I was just another innocent victim who they were trying to lure into their lifestyle of crime. Deep down I was becoming more and more unhappy. I started drinking more to forget the unhappiness that I was carrying inside.

I knew that my drinking was getting out of hand when I woke up in my bed one morning to find my face and hair covered in vomit. I hadn't even known I had been sick. I was lucky because I could have choked on my own vomit and died. This has happened to many alcoholics.

Every time I walked along Cricklewood Broadway I noticed that I was being followed. It was always the same man and one night he followed me right to my front door. As I opened the front door, he tried to push his way in. I was petrified and screamed for Natalie. 'Get out.' I shouted as him.

'I'll have you one day,' he said. I was scared to walk along the street late at night on my own. The only way for me to escape this was stay in the wine bar until the end of the night and get really drunk. I would then allow some of the male regulars to take me home for my protection. I knew that allowing men to stay the night just to protect me wasn't what I wanted, but it was an easier choice than being raped by this man. Life is hard for women on the streets, with no one to care for them.

"I was getting more involved in a dangerous lifestyle."

I was getting more involved in a dangerous lifestyle. I would get drunk to the point of blacking out and I knew many people in the pub were beginning to talk: 'Be careful Kelly', they would say.

I was part of a gang of drug dealers, murderers, people who had been in prison, prostitutes and pimps. Their main activities were stealing, fighting and dealing drugs. When the majority of people in the civilised world turn the lights out at night, there is another world just beginning and I was part of it. I would watch people being beaten and left for dead. It was scary stuff. The people I called friends had stone cold hearts.

One Sunday as I walked along the street, I spotted a church and stood and watched as people went in. They were all suited and booted and looked clean and tidy, with nice clothes and nice hair. For the first time since I left Scotland I stopped to take a look at myself: my hair was bleached blonde and I weighed twelve and a half stone. I wore an old black leather jacket, a black top and tatty old black trousers. My boots were worn out and split at the sides. I looked very rough. My breath smelt of alcohol and my clothes smelt of stale cigarette smoke. I was ashamed when I looked at myself. I felt that if I were to walk into the church everyone would turn around and stare. 'They will think I'm a tramp.' I thought to myself.

I realised that I was disgusted with the person that I was becoming. When I lived in Scotland I tried to keep myself smart, but now I only had the clothes I came to London with. 'But why should I bother to care about myself when no one else does?' I thought to myself. I knew that if Mum was alive she would care, but she wasn't. This thought made me more determined to give up on myself. I just wanted to die so that I could be with her.

Theresa was a regular at the pub. She lived in a back street flat, and was lonely, angry and fed up with life. As soon as the pub opened, Theresa would be there. She often asked people to stay with her at her flat because she was so lonely. One night when I was so drunk I could hardly walk, she said 'Please stay at mine'.

'Why not,' I thought. It was easier than getting one of the regulars to walk me home.

What a shock I had when I entered Theresa's flat. It was horrible, dark and smelly. There were bugs in the kitchen and bin bags everywhere. Empty drink bottles covered the worktops; empty cans and spoons were all over the floor. Old blankets hung across the window. Theresa told me that I could stay in her daughter's room where there were two beds. As I entered the child's room I was horrified at the smell: old sheets were spreads across the window and dirty ashtrays lay on the bed. The room was dark and cold with only a few broken toys in sight. A little girl lay on one of the beds. If I been a man I could have done anything to this child and I feared for her life.

Theresa allowed alcoholics and drug dealers to sleep in her daughter's room and I realised that she was at risk of being sexually abused. I was absolutely horrified that Theresa wasn't protecting her daughter. I felt sick at the sight of a child living such a cruel and horrible childhood.

As I climbed into the other bed, I wondered how this poor little girl's life would turn out. I had lived in a home with morals and discipline and my life was a mess, what possible hope did she have? I caught lice that night.

I got to know a friend of Theresa's called Bobby. He was Andrews's brother, but Andrew was too ashamed of him to tell anyone they were related. Bobby was a heroin addict and one day I asked him how he had ended up on the gear. His story was like so many other stories that I had heard.

Bobby hadn't wanted to leave Scotland but when his mother died his family fell apart and he came to London to find a job. He got sucked into a lifestyle that so many young people fall victim to: drugs, alcohol, and clubbing. He had a child but when he and his girlfriend split up, he never got to see his child because of his drug addiction.

He started off smoking dope and then moved on to stronger things. He ended up on cocaine and had to find ways of making money to feed his habit. In the end he became a rent boy in the West End and Hampstead Heath. It was the quickest and easiest way for him to make money. He told me that he hated himself and his life, and had tried to commit suicide on many occasions. He needed drugs to block his conscience and to forget about all the people he had wronged and all of the horrible things that he had done in order to survive.

Bobby and his friends would often sit in Theresa's flat smoking I would watch them and inhale the fumes. I was spending more time with the heroin addicts and had to be careful not to start taking heroin myself. I knew that I wouldn't cope with keeping up a job and a heroin habit.

Sunday night at the pub was karaoke night and I loved to go. There was a new crowd in the club and they began to talk to Theresa and me. They told us that they were from out of town and had come to London to work. One of them, a man named Brian, began to chat me up. He asked me if I would like to go out for a drink the following week. Normally I would have told him to get lost. 'I'm not sure,' I said, 'maybe I'll see you later in the week.' He was there again the following night, and the night after that. Each time he asked me out.

'What do you think?' I asked Theresa

'I'm not sure. Maybe a boyfriend is what you need to quieten you down.' Theresa convinced me there would be no harm in going for a drink so I suggested to Brian that we meet up in the park during the day, so I could suss him out. We met the following Thursday for half an hour. I still wasn't sure about him but I agreed to go for a drink on Friday night. We arranged to meet in the pub at 8 o'clock and I asked my friend Sophie to meet us at Hendon with her new boyfriend. Friday arrived and I was very nervous; I knew deep down that this guy wasn't for me.

I arrived at the pub and met Brian. Sophie said she would ring at 9 o'clock and ask me to come to Hendon. I was feeling uneasy and didn't want to drink much. Brian agreed to go to Hendon, so we phoned for a cab and went to meet Sophie and her boyfriend. I spent most of my time catching up with Sophie and didn't say much to Brian at all. I told Sophie I didn't like Brian and that he definitely wasn't my type. Sophie had had a few drinks and wanted to go home with her boyfriend.

When we left the pub at 11pm, I spoke to Brian and said I was really sorry but I wasn't interested in having a boyfriend right now and I hoped I hadn't wasted his evening. He took it really well, and offered to take me home in a cab. I was unsure, as Brian had made me feel uncomfortable but I agreed; it was only a lift home.

I had kept myself sober all night and I tried not to make conversation after we got into the cab. Brian asked a few questions about where I lived. I assumed it was for the cab driver so I told him that I shared a flat but my flatmate had gone away for the weekend. The cab pulled up outside my flat. 'Don't worry I'll pay your way,' he said.

'Thanks for a lift home,' I said.

I opened the taxi door and got out. I felt relieved to be safely at home. I kept looking back as I took my keys out. I was watching to see the cab drive off but it didn't. Suddenly Brian was behind me.

'What are you doing?' I asked, 'why aren't you going home in the cab?' An uneasy feeling washed me. 'How are you going to get home?' I asked nervously.

'I'll order another cab. I was hoping for a cup of tea,' he said.

'I'm tired I just want to go to bed,' I said but I felt bad about the fact that he had paid for the taxi and let him in for a quick cup of tea.

'It's cold and late,' he said 'I'll order a cab as soon as I get in.'

I put the kettle on and made a cup of tea; I heard him on the phone and was hoping the cab would come quickly. 'There's a cab office across the road', I said. I was starting to get annoyed with him and just wanted him to leave.

'Can I use your toilet?' he asked,

'Okay then' I said and went to my room. It had

"There was nowhere for me to escape to."

no lock so I stood there quietly waiting to hear the front door shut. A few minutes passed and I still hadn't heard the door. I now began to feel scared, as I wasn't sure what Brian was doing. I finally heard the toilet flush and hoped that he was on his way out. However, I heard my bedroom door open and he started moving closer to me. There was nowhere for me to escape to. He grabbed my face and tried to kiss me.

'No!' I began to say, 'I don't want this, please just go.'

I felt very intimidated. The look on his face had changed to one of anger. He grabbed me by the wrists and threw me onto the bed, then he began to try to kiss me. I clenched my lips together and moved my head side to side to try and avoid him. 'What is wrong with this man?' I thought. He pushed me hard on the bed. I was petrified; I didn't want him to beat me.

'You want this' he said. He began to pull his trousers off with one hand. He was becoming more forceful. I could smell alcohol on his breath and I realised that I was being raped. The flat was high above the shops so I knew my screams would not be heard. All I could say was help me.

The more I struggled the more aggressive he became. He was too strong and too heavy. I don't remember what happened after that. I must have passed out; my body couldn't take anymore.

When I came round he was standing by the bed with his clothes on. He said nothing. I was still in shock. I wanted to punch him, I opened my mouth to scream and shout but nothing come out. He turned his face away; he couldn't even look at me, 'You pig!' I said inside, 'I'll have you done for this'. I just stared at him as he left, I felt sicker than I ever had in my life.

I didn't know what to do. I looked in the mirror and saw that my face had turned white. I felt dirty and thought about having a bath. I decided against it as I had to go to the police and I knew a bath couldn't take the dirty feeling away.

I started wondering if people would blame me, or say that it was my fault. Where I grew up in Scotland, a girl was raped and people blamed her. They said it was her fault for inviting a man into her home. This raced through my mind and I wasn't sure if I'd done the same thing. I had let this man into my home and I wondered if what had happened was my fault in any way. I was so confused but I hadn't led him on or encouraged him in any way. I knew that I had been stupid to allow him into my flat but I hadn't asked for this. I hardly knew him; I didn't even know his surname.

I was afraid that people would see me as someone who was dirty. I had already been rejected by my dad and couldn't bear the thought of being rejected by my friends too. I needed to talk to someone to make sense of all that had happened.

I wanted to go to the police but I couldn't bear to go alone, as I knew they would have to examine my body. I needed someone to support me and thought I might be able to trust my friend Tina who worked at the pub.

I went to the pub. It was only eleven in the morning and they had just opened. I was in such a daze, the barmaid was shocked when she saw me and asked me if I was okay. When I shook my head to say no, she poured me a drink and sat down at the table. I was the only one in the pub. My stomach turned and I couldn't drink my drink.

As we sat there, I tried to work out if I could trust Tina. I was afraid she would tell all the regulars what had happened. They were the only friends I had and I didn't want them to know. I felt so ashamed of myself that I thought it best not to say anything. I left the pub and caught the bus home.

"I felt so ashamed of myself"

When I got back into my flat I ran the bath, although I knew that it couldn't wash away my hurt and pain. I wished I could just wash my life away. The bath didn't make me feel better. I felt clean until I stepped out of the water and then I felt dirtier than ever.

I stayed in bed all weekend, in shock and numb with pain, but I had to get up for work on Monday morning. I looked at my reflection in the mirror. My reflection showed a face that was hard; reflecting the fact that my heart was as hard as a stone.

As I walked down Cricklewood Broadway that Monday morning on my way to work, I hung my head in shame. I was now carrying the pain and anger of a rape victim and felt so dirty and ashamed. I was also angry with myself for not having the courage to go to the police and for allowing Brian to get away with what he had done to me.

I just wanted to bury the horrible nightmare deep down inside of me. I knew that the pain and shame of that awful night would be my secret and I would carry it with me for the rest of my life.

Brian was not seen again after that night. Theresa asked his work mates what had happened to him and they said that he'd left his job and moved back home.

After the rape I let myself go completely. My drinking became heavier and I asked Bobby to get me the drugs that he used just to block out his memories. I would often wake up in dirty flats with heroin addicts. I would sit in a daze inhaling the fumes whilst they would take their fix.

I had never been taught about heroin, I learned through experience. I also knew nothing about HIV or AIDS or how you caught them.

One of the heroin addicts, a man called Mickey, told me that he had AIDS and could die any day. He was so young and handsome that you couldn't tell he had AIDS by looking at him. People like Mickey no longer cared about themselves or anyone else; they continued taking drugs, drinking alcohol and having sex with anyone. Mickey told me that his uncle had sexually abused him when he was younger. His mother wouldn't believe him and his family disowned him as he grew older. He felt rejected and turned to drugs at a very young age. It was his way of escaping from the pain of the abuse he suffered and dealing with the fact that no one cared about him. He eventually ended up as a male prostitute.

It was heart breaking to watch a man completely destroyed by life. When I looked at my life I realised that I was better off that my friends who were drug addicts. I still had a job and a roof over my head, but I knew that if I continued living my life in the way I was, the chances were that I would end up in a similar situation to them. My future wasn't looking good and I had to pull myself together. I felt something inside telling me 'Don't give up, keep going.' I didn't know what it was, or even understand it, but I knew deep down that I had to keep going.

One night I was in the bar with Mickey, when a small, smartly dressed, good looking Italian man walked in. He started coming to the wine bar most nights and I found out that his name was Nicholas. Theresa had known him for a long time and he would go to Theresa's flat night after night. He felt sorry for her daughter and offered her money for shoes and clothes. He would often turn up with DVDs, drink and take away food, or he would offer us money and ask if we needed anything. We were amazed at his generosity and I began to wonder where he got all this money from. I soon discovered that he was a heroin dealer, but I believed that he had to be a decent person because of the way he cared for Theresa and her daughter.

One night at about 11:30pm I was getting ready to go to bed when the phone rang; it was Theresa. 'Nicholas is here and he wants you to come to my flat and have a drink.'

'Not tonight,' I said, 'I need some rest.'

'He'll be there in 15 minutes in a cab. Be ready.' I couldn't believe I was being ordered around and was annoyed. I got ready and waited.

'What's the matter?' I asked when Nicholas arrived.

'Nothing', Nicholas said, 'I just want you to come to Theresa's for a drink.' I wasn't in the mood but there was no point in arguing about it now.

I arrived and asked Theresa, 'What's this about?'

'It's Nicholas, he likes you.'

'I'm not interested,' I said. Theresa tried to convince me he was a great guy, but I wasn't interested in anything but friendship.

Nicholas phoned me one night: 'I need your help,' he said, 'I'm sure the police are watching me. Come in the cab until I do the drop off. It's safer if you're around, the police don't know you.' He was always good to us and I found it hard to say no to him. I agreed to keep a look out while he dropped off the drugs.

Another time I received a phone call from him saying he had a tip off that the police were following him and he had to make a collection that night. It was around 12:30am and I felt uneasy. I agreed to go with him but told him this would be the last time.

I'd had a few too many drinks and didn't know what I was doing. I went with Nick in the cab to collect the heroin. I was frightened when I realised that I would have gone to prison if we'd been caught and I said that I would never help again. I looked at the balls of heroin and thought about what it had done to Bobby and Mickey; it made me feel sick.

After the deal I just wanted to go home but instead Nicholas and I ended up at Theresa's drinking, He really liked me but I didn't feel the same as I didn't trust him. I knew that he didn't love me; he just wanted to lure me into his world, get me hooked on heroin and send me into a life of prostitution to make money for his drugs. He had done this to other girls.

"I knew that he didn't love me"

That night Nicholas stayed at my flat. We drank a lot and I ended up sleeping with him. The next morning I was horrified and wondered how I could have let it happen. I knew that Nicholas took heroin so there was a high risk he could have had AIDS. This was where alcohol had led me to. For many years I had wanted to be dead but not like this.

I plucked up the courage to ask Nicholas the truth. 'Do you have AIDS?'

'No,' he said. He was angry that I had asked him and left.

I was still scared. I didn't like Nicholas enough to sleep with him, so I couldn't understand why I had. My indulgence in smoking, drugs and alcohol had brought me to this place and I knew that it had to stop. It was frightening me; I would often drink so much that I'd black out and wake up the following morning covered in my own vomit. Now a drunken night with a heroin addict could cost me my life. This wasn't how I wanted my life to end. The following day I couldn't bear to put another drink to my mouth.

In the days that followed I was unable to get out of bed in order to go to work and I knew that it would only be a matter of time before I lost my job. After a few days I received a phone call from my boss, saying that they needed me back. I had to return to work so that I would be able to pay the rent; I didn't want to lose my flat.

I desperately needed to talk to my friend Tina so I returned to the wine bar. She hadn't been seen for a few days and the regulars were starting to get worried because this wasn't like Tina. We tried calling but she didn't respond. Two weeks later, a very pale and withdrawn Tina showed up at the wine bar.

'What has happened? Where have you been?' I asked.

Tina didn't want to talk about what had happened at first but she eventually opened up. She had been seeing a guy and went back to his flat where he locked her in and raped her. Someone eventually heard her screaming, called the police and the man was taken into custody. She asked for my support and I was happy to be there for her because I knew how she felt. I was still too ashamed to tell her my story though.

The trial was held at the Old Bailey and I went to court with Tina. The jury decided that she had entered the flat by her own will and the man was found not guilty. Tina was devastated 'Just because I went to his flat didn't mean I wanted to be beaten and raped!' she cried. Many women who are raped feel to ashamed to tell their stories and those that do are often not believed or made to feel that they are at fault in some way. Tina was scared for her life and afraid that she might meet the man again. We drowned our sorrows together.

Tina turned cold hearted and stopped caring; some nights she would get so drunk and sleep with men just for money. She suggested that I do it to but I refused.

I went to see Theresa as I'd been avoiding her flat because I didn't want to see Nicholas. When I arrived, Theresa said, 'I heard what happened between you and Nicholas. I hope you were careful, I heard he has AIDS.'

I went into shock. I was too afraid to go to the doctors to check if I had AIDS. I was petrified the answer would be 'yes' and I knew that if I found out I had AIDS it wouldn't be long before I ended up on heroin just like Bobby. I was angry with Theresa for encouraging me to go out with Nicholas; she was supposed to be my friend. I didn't want to fall out with her as we were both part of the same crowd but I knew I would never trust her again.

I began to hang out with Bobby and Mickey. One night Bobby and Theresa had an argument and she asked if Bobby and Mickey could stay at my flat. They bought some alcohol with them and began to smoke heroin. It smelt like death and I knew if Natalie came home and caught them she would hit the roof. I'm sure the fumes made me high and I went to bed, telling Bobby and Mickey to come in my room when they were finished. I fell asleep and woke up the next morning to find Bobby asleep on my bed; there was no sign of Mickey.

I came out of my room as Natalie was coming out of hers.

'Oh Mickey is so gorgeous isn't he?' she said.

I was horrified, 'You didn't sleep with him did you?' I asked.

She looked worried. 'Why? What's up?'

The words flew out my mouth: 'He has AIDS.'

The colour drained from Natalie's face and she couldn't speak. She ran to the toilet to be sick. She slept around every week, not realising the consequences. Was Natalie's life over too?

My relationship with Natalie fell apart after that because she was angry with me for bringing Mickey to the flat. Living together became a problem. I went to the pub and had a few drinks with my friend Stanley.

I first met Stanley on the day he was released from Wormwood Scrubs prison. He liked my smart and cheeky attitude and we became friends. It was always the high life with him, champagne and cocaine; I loved it. I was close to Stanley and looked upon him as a big brother. I always helped him out and he would do the same for me. I had once helped him with a robbery and he liked me because of that. Stanley spent his life stealing from factories, warehouses, shops and banks and he wanted me to work alongside him. I had been his watcher one time he broke into some lockups and though I loved the danger and excitement, a life in prison was not what I wanted.

My 21st birthday was only a few weeks away. I didn't have any money but liked the idea of having a party to cheer me up. I was delighted when the manager of the wine bar said I could hold the party there for free.

The wine bar was packed on the evening of my party and the music was pumping, but I wasn't happy. The place was full of drug dealers, prostitutes, armed robbers, fraudsters, drug addicts and alcoholics, many just out of prison. These hard-faced people were my friends; we lived in the same world, our attitudes and characters were the same. We had no future, no ambition, no hope whatsoever; we had all given up because we could see no way out. The only life we knew was alcohol, drugs, sex and the streets.

I saw a pub full of brave faces but deep down their hearts were broken. I knew that my face was the same: cold and hard with no love to be seen. I could never have imagined that the death of my mother would bring me to this place.

"I could never have imagined that the death of my mother would bring me to this place."

Stanley lived across the road from me, and I popped in to see him one night after work. It was the first time I had been in his flat and he asked if I liked it. He said that he was moving in with his girlfriend and asked if I wanted to rent it from him. Stanley said that everyone in the pub wanted his flat but he didn't trust any of them to pay the rent. He knew I worked hard every week and paid my rent which was why he wanted me to have it. I didn't like the idea because you had to walk down a long dark alley to get to the flat but Stanley plied me with more drinks and a spliff and managed to convince me to take it.

I arrived back at my flat and, looking at Natalie's angry face, I knew it would be best for me to move out. I didn't know then that this was the beginning of a much darker journey than I could have ever imagined.

A few days later I walked down the alley with my suitcase; it was more frightening than I had thought it would be and I couldn't wait to get in the door and up the stairs. When I got in to the flat it was disgusting. Stanley had left it in such a mess and the smell was absolutely awful. The only furniture was a dirty old mattress which had been left on the floor.

One of the rooms had housed two rottweilers and Stanley had locked them in and let them do their business in there. As I opened the door, my stomach began to heave. The next room I went into was the bathroom, when I pulled back the shower curtain, cockroaches crawled out from behind it. The kitchen was the worst: I picked up the rubbish bin and, to my horror, maggots spilled onto the floor. I looked in the oven, and as I opened the door, a mouse ran out.

The electricity suddenly went out. I felt awful, as if I had become nothing. I left the flat and locked the door not able to stand being there. The only place I had to go to was Theresa's; her flat wasn't much better but at least I wouldn't be alone.

I returned to my new flat fearing for my life. Surrounding me were heroin addicts desperate for me to take a fix. Prostitution, heroin and death were all I could see for my life.

Due to my loneliness and fear of living on my own, I entered into a violent relationship with a drug dealer. My life consisted of mental, verbal and physical abuse. He smashed up my flat and threatened to burn me out of it. I was living in the hands of another man's anger and rage and it was terrifying.

Frightened for my life, I closed my eyes, clenched my fists and screamed from deep inside me, 'If you are real God, save me! Send someone into my life to help me.'

A week later I met Paul. It was Saturday afternoon and Theresa was helping me to move an old bookshelf into the flat. Two young butchers were standing outside and one of them, a small Irish guy shouted, 'Do you need any help?' I found out his name was Paul and he lived in the flat a few doors along from me. He didn't look rough or nasty and I thought it would be nice to have a friend to talk to. Maybe he would even be able to help me get out of the life I was living.

That night he popped in for a drink. We sat down and started to chat and he began to roll a spliff; we got on really well and I really liked him. That night we got drunk and slept together. Once again I risked my life, I knew absolutely nothing about Paul, but I later found out that he was also a drug dealer. At that point, he was just a bloke I could have some fun with. As the weeks passed all we did was drink, smoke hash and take speed. It was fun to begin with, but our relationship took a turn for the worse as the drugs began to change our characters. Paul's behaviour changed; he became violent, abusive, jealous and controlling. I decided that I'd had enough and we went our separate ways for a few weeks but we got back together not long after.

Christmas was approaching and Theresa asked if I would like to spend Christmas day at her flat; she would cook dinner. I had loved Christmas when I was a child and the thought of spending the day alone was terrible. We decided to each put £20 towards dinner. Deep down I didn't want to go but I thought, as it was Christmas, Theresa would make an effort and have the place nice and clean.

"I had called out to God... and pleaded with him"

When I had finished work for Christmas I bought a big bottle of vodka and went home. Paul was still working and I told him to come up to the flat as soon as he finished. A few of his friends turned up too and I invited them in for a drink. My intention was to get completely drunk and drown my sorrows about spending Christmas in London when I really wanted to be in Scotland.

Christmas day at Theresa's was the worst I had ever spent. She had entered into a life of prostitution and had given up on herself and everything else. The flat was absolutely filthy; it had become a den for heroin addicts and alcoholics with empty beer cans spilling out of the bin all over the floor and old, burnt spoons lying around where they had been used by the addicts to burn their gear.

It was so disgusting that I couldn't bear to eat my dinner. I felt so sick of the life I was living; all I could see was misery. Theresa had tried her best so I didn't tell her how I felt, because I didn't want to upset her. When Paul came to meet me he was horrified at where I had had to spend Christmas. I felt so ashamed of my life.

It was the begining of a new year. My relationship with Paul was going well and we had been accepted by the in crowd. We spent all of our time nightclubbing, drinking and getting high on drugs. We decided to get engaged; finally something good was happening in my life.

One day the following Summer, a man in a suit knocked on the door and told me that I was living in the flat illegally. He said the council wanted to close the flats down as they were unfit to live in; they were crawling with mice and the alley way was infested with rats. I was given an eviction notice and had 28 days to leave. I had nowhere to go. Paul had recently moved in with me so he was going to be homeless too.

"I found out I was pregnant." The following week I got the biggest shock of my life: I found out I was pregnant. I was petrified, what sort of life could I give a child? I didn't know anything about being pregnant and I really needed my mum to talk to.

I didn't know where to go or who to turn to for help. Some friends advised me to go to the council so I took my eviction notice to them and they sent someone to see where I was living. Enviromental health inspected the flat, and wrote a report which said that I had to leave the flat as soon as possible as it was unfit to live in. Eventually I received a letter from them saying that they had found me a flat and they wanted me to view it.

The flat was in East Finchley; a place that I hadn't heard of before. I found my way to the address I'd been given and was horrified to find it was a high-rise block of council flats.

When I got inside the flat; it was filthy and there was a strong smell of urine. The council said that would put a new kitchen and bathroom in if I took it. I said yes, and moved in on December the 8th 1997.

I still had the worry of AIDS at the back of my mind and being pregnant, I had to face up to my biggest fear and have blood tests done. I was terrified, but my results came back clear; there was nothing wrong with the baby or me. It was the biggest relief in my life and the first miracle I had experienced. I had called out to God as soon as I had found out that I was pregnant and pleaded with him for my baby to be okay. I left the hospital crying with joy.

I had recently found out that Nicholas now had full blown AIDS and felt that I'd been given a second chance at life. Everything seemed to be going well and I didn't want to touch drugs or alcohol ever again.

I was working through my pregnancy, trying to make the flat nice for the baby. Paul was working on the flat too as he was currently unemployed. He was fed up with life and spent most of the time smoking dope. I was clean for the first time in eight years and wanted everything to be perfect; I wanted my baby to have a life filled with love.

> *"Everything seemed to be going well and I didn't want to touch drugs or alcohol ever again. "*

As my due date approached, Paul and I began to argue. I asked him to stop smoking dope but he didn't want to and the arguments got worse. I was scared to have a baby all on my own because I didn't have a clue about what to do with a baby. I told Paul that I really needed him at this point in my life. I really missed my mum. I wanted to be just like her and do the best that I could.

In March 1998 I gave birth to a beautiful baby boy. I cried when I saw him; I was holding a real live miracle in my arms. I knew that Paul and I were the only family this baby had and it was down to us to love and protect him. When the baby and I came home from hospital, I was angry to see Paul smoking dope. I didn't want him to do that around my child.

Things got worse when my in-laws arrived from Ireland. The baby had been born by caesarean section and I needed help to take care of the baby and rest after the operation, but they expected me to look after them. They would shout, swear and tell lies about me. This caused me so much pain especially when Paul joined in with them

Paul and I began to argue more. We would fight and sometimes he became violent. I had tried so hard to make a new life for myself but I was now living in an abusive relationship. I asked Paul to leave and became a single mum.

Being a single mum really petrified me. I lived with the fear that I wouldn't be able to provide a good life for my child. I felt like a failure and was very embarrassed about being a single mother. At this point, I was hurt and angry with my life.

I was determined that I would never go back to drugs and alcohol. As the weeks passed I loved living on my own with the baby in the peace and quiet. There was no more shouting and fighting. My employers understood my situation and let me return to work a couple of months early with my baby.

I had kept my life straight during my pregnancy and after my baby was born, but now it was to take an unexpected turn. I received a phone call from Annie, a friend in Scotland who wanted to come to London to work. 'That's great' I thought, 'I'll have a real friend.'

Annie got a job just outside of London and asked if she could stay with me at the weekends. I agreed happily. On the first weekend she bought some cider and cigarettes with her. I had stayed sober almost a year, but that weekend I got really drunk and ended up vomiting the whole night.

Annie was a few years younger than me and was looking for fun. Every weekend she came to stay we would end up drinking. I felt under a great deal of stress raising a child on my own, I was also receiving threatening phone calls from Paul's family. The lies and abuse became too much for me to handle and once again, I needed an escape. I was back at work, which meant that I had money to spend on alcohol.

There was a pub around the corner from the block of flats where I lived. As it was summertime, people sitting outside would call Annie and I over for a chat when we walked by. They would ask if we wanted a drink and we decided to join them. At first we made up stories about who we were and I'm sure that we came across as very full of ourselves. The pub was the only exciting place in the area and it was nice to be receiving so much attention. However, what started out as harmless fun soon turned into my worst nightmare.

Annie left her job because she was fed up with it and asked if she could come live with me. She was a qualified nanny and offered to babysit for me to pay her way. I thought this was a great idea; at last I had someone to help me. A few of the girls from the pub had asked me to go out for a drink with them on Friday nights and I was now able to.

When I got to the pub, everyone was delighted to see me. A lot of the regulars had plenty of money and were happy to buy drinks for me because I was new and exciting. I found myself becoming part of the in crowd and before I knew it I was taking cocaine. I hadn't been able to afford it before but now I was being given it for free, a lot of it. Cocaine would numb the hurt and pain I felt, it also helped me to forget about Paul, who I still loved deep down.

I found myself in a downward spiral. The more cocaine I took, the more I wanted. Without even realising it, I had become an addict. I started taking it morning, afternoon and evening; my appetite disappeared and I lost a lot of weight, all I wanted was another hit of cocaine. I started turning up late for work and sometimes wouldn't even bother going in. One day my boss told me not to bother coming in again. Unsure of where to turn, I contacted Paul but he was in no position to help me as he was on crack cocaine. Once again, I had no one.

It was nearly Christmas. I asked Annie if she would stay in London with me, as it was the baby's first Christmas and I wanted it to be nice. She agreed but a week later changed her mind because she wanted to go home to Scotland for Christmas. I was angry with her because, deep down, I would have loved to be able to go home to Scotland too.

Without my job, my only income was my social security benefit. Several of the men in the pub knew that I'd lost my job and started offering my cocaine. I took it gladly, but soon needed more. At this point they asked me for sex in return for money. I had promised myself that I would never sleep with someone for money, no matter how low I got, but now prostitution seemed to be my only option.

The evening that I decided to do it, I got dressed up and headed to the pub; I was a nervous wreck. I was so ashamed about what I was planning to do that I used the small amount of money I had to buy cocaine. I needed to feel completely numb before I could go ahead with it.

That night I handed myself over to prostitution. I looked at my face in the mirror, it was completely different and I started to feel sick. When the man put the money in my hand I felt that the life in me had been taken away.

I made enough money to buy myself a ticket to Scotland. I went to visit Paul before I left; he was hooked on crack and had become a complete mess. I suggested that he returned to Ireland. I returned to Scotland that Christmas, hoping to find the person I used to be, but I realised that Scotland couldn't change my life at this point.

I arrived back in London on New Years Eve and I went to a party. Everyone there was high on drugs, and I began to smoke cocaine which was a different high to snorting it. I saw a man, high on drugs, beat up his girlfriend, but I was so high that I couldnt move to help her. The next day I was discusted with myself. I was frightened by how high I had been and realised that my life was completely out of control.

The next morning I decided that I didn't want to live like that again and I cried out to God: 'Please take away this cocaine addiction and the prostitution.'

"I cried out to God"

I looked in the mirror; my mouth was covered in cold sores, I weighed only seven stone and my body was sore. I spoke to Paul and we decided I should go with him to Ireland so that we could talk and try to sort things out. We really did love each other, but we just broke each other's hearts.

As I went outside that day I met a Scottish lady who lived in the same block of flats. She told me that she had seen me walking in and out of the pub for months. She said, 'That's not the life you really want'.

'I know', I said, 'I'm heading to Ireland tomorrow to leave that life behind.'

I arrived in Ireland and ended up being rushed to hospital. I was in so much pain; it felt like a knife was ripping through my stomach. I was screaming in agony and I thought I was going to die. I began to throw up black stuff, like tar. The doctor did some blood tests but they couldn't find anything wrong with me. There was no medical explanation for what had happened.

Later on in life I realised that God had taken me through deliverance. I had cried out to Him to set me free from my cocaine addiction and from prostitution and that's exactly what He did; he cleared all the rubbish out of my system. After that day I never again craved cocaine, the addiction was completely gone. I was free.

I wasn't happy in Ireland. I didn't get on with Paul's family; they would talk about me behind my back and call me names. I needed to be around people who loved me and accepted me, but none of them could see that and I felt rejected. I wanted to talk about what I'd been through; the cocaine addiction and the prostitution but I was too ashamed and afraid of being rejected.

I had to depend on Paul because I had no money, which made me feel like a prisoner trapped in a life I hated. I started to fall into depression. Every time I had been desperate I had cried out to God and he'd listened. I cried out once again: 'Please get me out of Ireland.'

News had spread in the village that a faith healer had come to pray for people. Apparently he was a Christian and people would come from all over the area for him to pray with them. Paul and I were invited to go and see him. I arrived at his home and he took me into a room and prayed for me. When he had finished he told me that Jesus had chosen me to look after Paul. I didn't have a clue what he meant and I thought it was strange. Paul went after me and when he came out of the room he looked pretty shaken. 'What did he say?' I asked. He told me that the man had told him to take his family out of Ireland as fast as he could.

My heart was jumping with joy! I couldn't believe what I was hearing. 'Wow,' I thought, 'God really does work in mysterious ways!' A week later Paul had got the money together and we went back to London.

I was so pleased to have my little family back together and decided that it would be a new start for all of us. I felt free for the first time in ages. However, some weeks later Paul began to go back to his old ways. He started drinking and smoking drugs again which resulted in him becoming abusive. I lived in fear lived of fighting and abuse. Neighbours were concerned and would knock on the door when they heard Paul shouting and swearing at me.

I tried my best; the house was always clean and there was dinner on the table, but it didn't matter what I did, it was never good enough. I would curl up on my bed and cry; I just couldn't bear it. I was becoming so depressed that my confidence was completely gone. When I had to go out my head hung in shame. I hated bumping into anyone I knew from the pub, because they knew my past so I began to stay in the flat, only leaving to buy food.

I began smoking 40 cigarettes a day in an attempt to forget my guilt, Week in week out my life was the same, the only thing I had to look forward to every week was my benefit cheque.

One night, unable to take any more, I decided to end my life. I just wanted to get away from the misery, heartache and abuse that I lived with and the guilt I felt about my past. I loved my son with all my heart, he meant everything to me but I had started to believe all of the lies I'd been told and thought that I was a complete failure, good for nothing. I wrote a suicide note and took a knife in my right hand and was about to push it into my wrist when I heard a voice say 'No, don't do it. Your son needs his mother.' Those words were true. I let the knife fall. How could I even contemplate doing such a thing? How could I take my life and leave my son without a mother? I went to my son, picked him up and held him tightly in my arms, silently begging his forgiveness for what I had tried to do.

"I wrote a suicide note and took a knife in my right hand"

I shared with a friend how I didn't want to live anymore and she suggested that I went to the doctors. The minute the doctor asked me what was wrong I started to cry. She said that I was suffering from depression and prescribed me anti-depressants. The first time I took the pills I felt sick and had to stay in bed. They took all of my energy away and actually made me feel worse. I didn't feel that they were doing me any good.

A few days later there was a knock on my door, it was my neighbour from downstairs. He said that he had watched me out the window drunk and fighting until blood was shed months ago and that as he watched me he prayed for me. He said he had called to ask if we would like to go to church on Sunday. I only thought about it for a minute before I agreed. It had been years since I had last gone to church and I thought it would be a good idea. Paul wasn't sure but I managed to persuade him.

I knew nothing about this neighbour but I had a feeling that God had sent him to help me. Sunday came and I got dressed up because that was how I remembered church as a child. We arrived at the church and it was very different to what I had imagined. Everyone was down to earth, wearing jeans and casual clothes. I liked that straight away. You didn't need to get dressed up, but were accepted just the way you were. The music was lively and everyone was singing and clapping. I liked the atmosphere and felt very safe there. For the first time in a long while, I didn't feel that I needed to watch my back. When the music finished I sat down and the preacher began to speak.

"I had a feeling that God had sent (my neighbour) to help me."

He said, 'Jesus loves you.' Those were the only words I took in. He said, 'Accept Jesus Christ as your Lord and Saviour.'

I accepted him straight away. I opened my heart to him and said. 'God I am sorry for everything I've done. Please help me. You're the only one who can.' I meant those words from the deepest part of my heart and when I said them I felt as if my whole insides had exploded. It was the most overwhelming feeling I had ever experienced. I felt a love like I'd never felt before; as if there was something sweeping over my whole body. I began to sob my heart out, I couldn't stop so I got up and went to the toilet. As I stood looking in the mirror, I no longer saw any guilt or shame, I felt like a little girl again. I felt free; I felt clean; I felt like a new person

My tears were still overflowing when I returned to my seat. Paul punched my arm. 'Stop it.' He said, 'Everyone is looking it's embarrassing.' I couldn't stop though; it was the best experience of my whole life. I had accepted Jesus Christ as my Lord and Saviour and now I was accepted and loved for who I was. I knew that Jesus loved me.

It was so real. I had received my salvation, my guilt and shame were gone and I had been forgiven for all I had done. As I lay in bed that night I felt wonderful. I had been given a second chance; a new life.

The next morning I threw my anti-depressant tablets away. I knew that I didn't need them anymore. My body was full of life, the heavy feeling I had had was gone. When I looked in the mirror I saw the real me for the very first time and I liked what I saw. My eyes had been opened.

I was enjoying my new life. I felt that I'd been freed from my past and was rebuilding my life in a positive way. I made new friends who surrounded me with so much love and encouragement; friends who I could trust and relax with, friends who wanted nothing but good for my life.

My days of being hard and of watching my back were over. I took driving lessons and managed to pass my driving test. Paul and I were married and we had three more children; I finally had a family of my own which was something I'd always wanted.

I started a new job and began to do some of the things that I'd always dreamed of doing. I had always wanted to travel and to see the world and went on some of the wonderful holidays that I had so longed for as a child.

I began to repair broken relationships with Paul's family and found my sister with whom I'd lost contact.

I went through a process of deliverence from my cigarette smoking. Anger, grief and depression were all taken from me. I loved every minute of my new life and I also started to love myself. I was happy and content inside; I had inner peace and joy in my life at long last.

Unfortunately at that time Paul didn't understand my experience. I told him that Jesus Christ was real but he would not listen. He started smoking weed and hash again and it wasn't long before he became addicted to cocaine and crack. From there he ended up on heroin and I knew that he was no longer in control of his life.

I had to watch him throw his life away. Some nights he didn't come home and I knew that he spent many nights out on the streets with drug dealers and prostitutes. Watching his anger and rage as he came down from the drug high was terrifying. I called out to God because He was my only hope. My prayers had now become tears overflowing from my inner being. I asked Jesus to hold my hand and to help me through it, and that's exactly what He did.

Days later I had an amazing dream. I saw Jesus Christ standing holding out His hand towards me. I prayed for an explanation and I felt God say to me: 'Tell everyone on the streets I love them and I am their only hope.' I was blown away by this; it was amazing. I knew after this that I must not give up on Paul.

One day I found out that Paul had committed adultery on several occasions including with prostitutes. Anger and hurt filled me just as they had when Mum died. I had allowed anger and unforgiveness to take over once and it had nearly cost me my life, I didn't want that to happen again. This time, in my pain, I ran straight into the arms of Jesus Christ, the Healer of broken hearts. He intervened; my anger and hurt was taken away and I became more loving and compassionate towards my husband despite what he was doing.

The situation became so bad that Paul lost everything we had worked so hard for. He then told me that he was going to Ireland, leaving me to cope on my own with four children. We had no money to pay the bills and the electricity was about to be cut off. Our house was about to be repossessed and we were facing homelessness. In the face of all this I cried out to God to save my family. I prayed that He would bring my husband out of the pit he was in.

My prayers were answered. A few weeks later Paul returned home, a broken man. Whereas before he had mocked me about my relationship with God, he now realised that only God could help him. It had been so difficult for me to cope with everything he had said and done to me but on that day the Lord spoke to me very clearly: 'Forgive your husband'.

'Please Lord Jesus, I need you to show me how to forgive him and love him.' I cried. The minute I prayed that prayer I felt something change inside. The lack of forgiveness just disappeared. I felt a love for Paul that I never thought I would ever feel again.

"My prayers were answered."

There was absolutely nothing that I could do to help Paul out of the mess he was in, but I knew that Jesus Christ could.

Paul had an amazing encounter with God and we discovered the extent of what Jesus Christ can do. When I began to pray for Paul, a lump of jelly came out of his mouth; this was his first deliverance. The jelly was the addiction from crack cocaine being removed from his body.

I then started to pray for the heroin addiction to be removed and Paul began to be sick. As he received Jesus Christ into his life, a shiver went right through his body; he had been touched by God.

Paul is now beginning, with a lot of love and support, to rebuild a broken life and to walk a new journey in with God. His life is a work in progress and is in God's hands.

His deliverance from heroin and crack cocaine is a real miracle. Deliverance is when we call out to God and by his Holy Spirit, he sets us free.

Part Three

Getting rid of the old baggage

When I arrived in London I came with a suitcase full of baggage. Baggage inside of me that only I could feel: rejection, anger, hurt, hatred, and abandonment. The more I did wrong, the more baggage I collected. The heavier it got the more strength I needed to carry it. I looked for ways to get rid of the baggage: alcohol, sex, drugs, but no matter how much I drank or how high I got the baggage was still there, rape, violence, abuse, prostitution. This baggage led me into a cruel, dark and dangerous world.

Throughout my life in London I was victimised, traumatised and violently abused. I had been dragged down alleyways, had my head smashed against brick walls, been punched and kicked to the floor. I was told I was worthless, no good, and a nobody. I was called every name you could imagine. I accepted this and I believed it was true. I endured violent abuse, as I believed I deserved it. But Jesus Christ took me out of it and showed me that no matter what I had done or who I had become, I wasn't a nobody I was a somebody.

I thought that changing my image would make me feel like someone different but it never did. It never changed who I was deep down inside. I bleached my hair blonde and plastered my face with make-up. I wore a mask because I didn't want anyone to see the real me. The tougher life got the more make-up I wore. You could always tell when I was having a really bad day, as my make-up would be heavier.

When I accepted Jesus Christ into my life I cried out for Him to clear all this baggage out, starting with the most painful part, the death of my mum. Tears streamed down my face as He dealt with the pain and I felt something happening deep down inside. They were tears of healing. The broken heart I had carried for so long was finally healed. Only Jesus Christ can heal a broken heart. I felt free for the first time in my life.

I can say with all truth and honesty that Jesus Christ gave me a new life. He gave me all that I had been looking for in alcohol, drugs, and men. I no longer hang my head in shame, instead I can hold my head up high. I have learned to love those who hurt me; I have forgiven the man who raped me and the man who sexually abused me.

God has also restored my relationship with my dad. I phoned him and I told him that I loved him and I was sorry. He told me that he was sorry too and that he loved me.

I had taken out all of my anger on him and none of it was his fault. He didn't know how I felt deep down or about the life that I'd been living. The death of my mum and the grief we all shared had ripped our family apart, but God has intervened and restored a great love between us.

Today my dad is my best friend. He has supported me through my new journey with Christ every single step of the way.

God has changed my life. I am a testimony to His transforming love and redeeming grace. I know that I'm not perfect; I am still a work in progress. But I am on an exciting journey!

I have been clean from drugs for eleven years now. If someone were to offer to me one million pounds I would never turn back. When my mum died I really just felt like it was the end of the world. But looking back, I realise it was part of God's plan. He wanted me to learn about a world that I would otherwise have not known existed, so that I could go and bring his love and hope to the broken hearted.

'The fruit of God's spirit is love, joy, peace, longsuffering, kindness, goodness, faithfulness, gentleness and self control.'

Galatians 5:22

That is what I have living in me.

Is Satan real?

Have you ever asked yourself if God is real? Have you ever asked yourself if Satan is real? I know that he is real because I have lived in his world. I had his spirit living in me; I lived under his control. When my mum died I said in my heart that there was no God. I allowed Satan's spirit to come into me. Satan's world is full of darkness; he allows a life that is held in bondage, slavery and sin, a life from which some people never escape. I attempted to keep control of my life but much as I tried, I couldn't and I would often find myself in dangerous situations. Satan's deception can come through alcohol and drugs. When I was on cocaine it was Satan's way of numbing my brain so that his spirit would have control. Satan's job is to kill, steal and destroy lives, his aim to destroy people. Alcoholics, drug addicts and many people with AIDS are under his control. People want to know why so many evil things happen, it's because Satan's spirit is real.

There are two worlds (God's world and Satan's world) and one choice. God has given us the free will to make that choice. The only way to defeat Satan in your life is to repent fully and allow God's spirit to live in you and transform you. It was no one's fault that my life turned out the way it did through my anger, which led me into Satan's world.

Who is this God who loved me so much?

'For God so loved the world that he gave his only begotten son, that whoever believes in him should not perish but have everlasting life. For God did not send his son into the world to condemn the world, but the world through him might be saved.'

John 3:16

I wondered what being a Christian was really about. Going to church every week wasn't enough for me. I got on my knees and asked God, 'Why am I here? Is it just to cook and clean, work, and look after my family? Is this what Christian life is all about?'

'Call to me and I will show you great and mighty things.'

Jeremiah 3:33

That is exactly what He did. Whilst on my knees, God gave me a vision. He showed me the streets of London and told me to go out and save the souls of the broken hearted. He also told me that I would write a book about my life. It would be called 'Brave Faces with Broken Hearts.' I laughed because I was always bottom of the class in school and my spelling was atrocious.

God showed me that He wanted me to reach out with His love to the many people who are hurting and dying on the streets of London: the prostitutes, drug addicts, and homeless people with AIDS. I have to tell them the Good News that Jesus Christ loves them too and that no matter what they have done they can be set free.

I decided to go to Bible School in Notting Hill Gate as I needed to find out for myself what the Bible and Christianity were all about. I discovered the answers that I had been searching for my whole life. Life finally made sense. There is a God who is real and who loves me. Satan is also real.

I now felt strong enough to go back out onto the streets of London, back to a cruel, dark world that I once lived in. I was going back as a completely new and transformed person. This time I had hope to bring.

London is a great city, full of life and excitement but there is also a dark side to the city that is cruel and dangerous; a part of the city that most people fear. Many people living in London have become victims of the life that I once led.

I arrived in London hoping to make a better life for myself but found myself trapped in a cruel and dangerous lifestyle that so many people are still trapped in with no way out and no hope. This is a life that ends in death for many people.

During the last three years I have gone out onto the streets of London; to the homeless, to prostitutes and to drug addicts. I have taken them food and gifts but the biggest gift I offer is the Good News of the Gospel of Jesus Christ. I tell them if he can change my life, he can change theirs too I have talked to prostitutes and watched tears stream down their faces as the spirit of God touches them.

As I walk through the West End and the suburbs I see people in sleeping bags, huddled in shop doorways, a can of beer and a tatty old bag with their few belongings stuffed inside by their sides. These cold, damp, miserable doorways are their bed for the night; the only place that they have to go.

In certain parts of the city, men and women line the streets selling their bodies. Desperate for money, they are living a life of prostitution, which they cannot see a way out of. The sadness sweeps across their faces, although this is often masked by a hardness that they use to protect themselves. Their hearts have become so cold and hardened by the lack of love they have been shown.

When I move amongst them; acknowledging them, talking to them and offering them food and gifts they respond so warmly and their joy is overwhelming. They are so grateful for what they are given, and truly thankful that their lives are truly touched.

I look at the faces of the women, full of heartache and desperation. Some walk with their heads hung down in shame, trying to hide the black eyes from their most recent beating. There are many women living at the hands of abuse; they are beaten and battered with nowhere to go. They push babies in pushchairs and cling tightly to the hands of their children as they search for safety but there is none to be found. They run into the arms of men looking for refuge and safety only to find themselves at the mercy of a man as violent and abusive as the last.

Children are living in the homes of drug addicts, they are subjected to violence and sexual abuse. They wonder the streets, so young and vulnerable, so desperate for money to escape their lives of poverty and so eager to escape from their unhappy homes that they fall straight into the hands of drug dealers. These innocent children start running drugs on the streets and before they realise it they've become victims of a dark, cruel world. Looking for love, their lives end in disaster

HIV AIDS is a deadly disease that is spreading rapid across the city. Men and women sleep around, looking for love and acceptance, only to end up with this awful disease. Many refuse to discuss, or even accept that they have it for fear that they will be rejected by friends and family or face the fact that their lives are over.

AIDS is a subject that many are afraid to bring up. Thousands are affected by it; many beautiful women and handsome men whose good looks are a deception along with a huge number of people living out on the streets.

There are heroin and crack dens all over the city; full of people trying to escape from the tragedy that their lives have become. Alone and afraid, they are the outcasts of society. People are afraid to talk to them, to even look at them. Some of these people have never been shown real love; they are victims of sexual abuse, rape and violence. Betrayed and rejected, their hearts are truly broken but deep down they are no different to you or me.

Many young prostitutes come to London to escape unhappy lives. Tragedy has often stuck their homes, often the loss of a parent. They are looking for love, refuge and safety, something to comfort them in their pain. However they become vulnerable victims at the hands of men who make them false promises, who tell them that they love them, and then send them out onto the streets as working girls to earn money for their pimp's drug addictions.

Poverty is on the increase. Many drug dealers, who have been in and out of prison since they were young, see selling drugs as the only way that they can make ends meet. No-one will employ them and they use any means possible to survive.

Many people on the streets can't afford clothes and shoes for their children and they are being sent out by their own parents to steal items.

Each time I went out onto the streets I found it more heartbreaking. I felt so helpless and knew that bringing food and gifts and listening to their heart-wrenching stories wasn't enough. God laid it on my heart that these people needed to be given hope. They needed a House of Hope.

For the last year I have rented a big house and this has become my first House of Hope. The house is a refuge; a place of safety where many come and go. The foundation is built on Jesus Christ.

Many people come for prayer; they ask for deliverance and to be set free. Heroin addicts, crack addicts, people just out of prison, rape victims, people suffering with grief and depression, homeless people, mental hospital patients both rich and poor have all come looking for deliverance from their own personal circumstances. Many have stayed, some longer than others and have moved on when they are ready to do so.

We have fed them, housed them and clothed them, but most importantly I have told them about God's love and how He is the only way out of their troubles. Everyone who has come to the house has had their own encounter with God.

Everything we do is committed to God in prayer and we watch the amazing work of God. Money and clothes have always been available when needed. Those who leave always keep in touch; we have become a family. When people return to visit it's great to see their progress and share their experiences of their new journey.

The need for the House of Hope is growing ; there are so many people looking for refuge and safety, so many people out on the streets with good hearts who have fallen victim to a cruel life through a broken heart.

It is by God's amazing grace that I am alive today to tell my story.

All proceeds from this book will go to support the House of Hope in London. Thank you for buying a copy; by doing so you are helping to feed, clothe, house and save the lives of many broken hearted people.

God bless you.

If you have been touched by what you have read and want to receive Jesus Christ as your Lord and Saviour please say this prayer:

Dear Lord Jesus

I believe you are the Son of God;
I believe you are the Saviour of the world.
You gave your life upon a cross to save me from my sins.
I ask you to forgive me for all the wrongs I have done.
I am truly sorry.
I now ask you to come into my life.
Be my Lord and Saviour.
Cleanse me and set me free.
I give my life back to you.
I will serve you in complete obedience
for the remaining days of my life.
Amen

If you have said this prayer, congratulations. You are now a brother or sister in Christ.

'God is our refuge and strength.
An ever-present help in trouble.'

Psalm 46:1